"I gave him a check, put her under my coat . . . and brought her home. I had found my poodle. Of course, deep down, I knew it was the other way around. That poodle had sat in that cage for a week or more just casing parents. She had found me!"

And so begins the great love affair between Josephine, an unregistered but magnificently-coated French poodle, and her best-selling authoress-owner.

Of course, in every romantic relationship one partner dominates, and Josie's authority was never disputed for a moment. Even Jackie's dog-hating husband, Irving Mansfield, was forced to submit to Josie's canine charms.

In the wonderfully warm and witty style which has made her last two books all-time international bestsellers, Jacqueline Susann writes the true story of the kookiest Manhattan "ménage à trois" ever!

Every Night, Josephine!

by JACQUELINE SUSANN

With an Epilogue by the Author

A NATIONAL GENERAL COMPANY

EVERY NIGHT, JOSEPHINE!
*A Bantam Book / published by arrangement with
Jacqueline Susann*

PRINTING HISTORY
*Geis edition published 1963
Bantam edition published February 1970
2nd printing
3rd printing
4th printing
5th printing
6th printing
7th printing
8th printing*

*Bantam Books are published by Bantam Books, Inc., a National
General Company. Its trade-mark, consisting of the words "Bantam
Books" and the portrayal of a bantam, is registered in the United
States Patent Office and in other countries. Marca Registrada.
Bantam Books, Inc., 666 Fifth Avenue, New York, N.Y. 10019.*

PRINTED IN THE UNITED STATES OF AMERICA

To Josephine
The Only Female with Whom
I Gladly Share My Husband's Love

CONTENTS

1

The Facts

I GOT UP at dawn to turn on the TV set. Josephine stared at me as if I was some kind of a nut. It was February 20, 1962. Colonel John Glenn hurtled into space and the nation held its breath and kept a marathon vigil. Josephine merely gave it a fast glance, yawned, and went back to sleep.

Because Josephine knows it's all a waste of time, money, and effort. Another country can't harm us. Getting into space won't help us. Because we are already doomed—soon to be enslaved by the new Master Race. And Josephine is a card-carrying member of this Master Race—the Master Race that is slowly conquering us all and will soon inherit the earth.

Small wonder that Josephine and her fellow members sit idly by and allow us to tinker with rockets and atom bombs. Josephine knows it takes more than bombs and rockets to conquer. The Master Race is equipped with a superior intelligence. They conquer with love and affection.

At this very moment they are infiltrating into every large city in the United States and Europe. A few have even slipped behind the Iron Curtain.

They appear in diplomatic drawing rooms, eavesdrop on top-secret conferences, and it is openly whispered in Washington that one, a raven-haired beauty, often shares the boudoir of a well-known senator.

So forget the bomb . . . the race for space. It's too late. We've all been taken. I know I have. And the odd part is, I don't care. I never even put up a fight. Like all the others, I walk around with a silly, simpering smile. A willing captive of a small member of the new Master Race. The French Poodle.

Maybe you think you'll escape! You're a born dog-hater. You're impervious to their sneaky charm. They can't get to you.

Want to bet?

Take my husband, Irving Mansfield. He was born in Brooklyn, has a college degree, is a creative television producer, brilliantly imaginative and commercially successful. He served in the Air Force in World War II. He has engaged in hand-to-hand combat with Madison Avenue advertising agencies, cosmetic sponsors, and even the Musicians Union. He survived two ulcers and five years' "close association" with Arthur Godfrey. So you see he's a real commando type. Definitely not the type to be taken over by a small French Poodle.

If you check his childhood background, he comes through clean, without one tendency toward subjugation. No early dog affiliations. No boyish romps with Spot or Rover. And not one person in his neighborhood was ever a regular at the Westminster Dog Show. He does admit that every now and then a sparse-looking dog did make an occasional appearance on the block. But it was no French Poodle. Why, if anything remotely resembling a French Poodle had ever appeared, his mother would have cooked it.

That's how it was with Irving and dogs when he was a boy. When he grew up, moved to Manhattan, went to college, and became the man he is today, he went through a dry period without seeing a dog for years. Oh, once in awhile, when he entered "21" or Sardi's, he did notice a small furry object with a jeweled collar checked in the coatroom. But it never entered his consciousness that *this* was a dog.

My own childhood experiences with dogs were equally barren. I was raised in suburban Philadelphia and had the misfortune to know some little girls whose fathers must have owned oil wells or were members of the Capone mob, because these miserable little creatures sported Shetland ponies. So you can see where my sights were set. I remember throwing fits and traumas for an entire week to gain my point and a pony. I came out fairly victorious. I settled for a Persian cat.

I liked that cat and devoted two full weeks of my life to it. Then one day, without so much as an "I'll-be-seeing-you," it took to the road in pursuit of a most unattractive lady cat. I guess they lived happily ever after, because I never saw either of them again. I was so crushed at this rejection that I switched my affection from the Animal Kingdom to a plump boy named Herman, who stared at me as if I were The Real Miss America. And that's how I spent my childhood. No stray dog or cat ever followed me home. Just Herman —or some equally fascinating replacement.

When I came to New York, I came as a young aspiring actress. And everyone knows, young aspiring actresses do more walking than acting the first few years. From nine till five they cover every producer's and agent's office in town.

So you can see that the extracurricular activity of walking a dog never entered my mind. And when I did get going in my career and had time to devote to a dog, I met Irving.

And there you have it. A full summation of Irving and me. No childhood exposure to the breed. No latent weaknesses. Two adults—strong-minded, steeped in togetherness, compatible in careers, confirmed hotel dwellers, commuters between New York and California. We had everything. All right—maybe we needed extra closet space, more sleep, a larger kitchen.

But the one thing we didn't need was a French Poodle.

2

How I Got Hooked

I WOULD LIKE to be able to say it was just an accident —or fate. Like I was taking a walk and a stray poodle just happened to follow me home. But to begin with, stray poodles do not roam up and down Central Park South. And if a stray poodle did follow me home, it would immediately be followed by a hysterical owner and the police. So remember, whenever you see a poodle dragging some captive around on a leash, it's the captive who put his own head in the noose. Because a poodle never goes in search of its victim. The victim goes in search of a poodle.

To any smug individual who as yet does not share his worldly goods with a poodle—who *knows* it will never happen to him—I offer just two words of advice.

WATCH OUT!

It sneaks up on you. The most innocent little incident can trigger it off, and wham! suddenly you get the "call." The insatiable urge to give up all worldly pleasures and donate your life to the care and raising of a French Poodle.

It happened to me on a day that was like any other day. I had been lunching with my good friend Dorothy Strelsin. Late in the afternoon we went back to her apartment. She wanted me to see some new pictures she had acquired. The moment she opened the door, a small furry object rushed to greet her, prancing on its hind legs in sheer ecstasy.

"This is Tinker," Dorothy said in a tender voice.

Then she picked up three pounds of squirming, elated dog, which immediately started to saturate her with adoring kisses. I stood by silently while Dorothy received five minutes of this rapturous affection. Then she placed him on the floor, and we entered the living room with Tinker capering at her heels, squealing with joy at her mere presence. Her husband, Alfred, looked up from his paper and said, "Hello, dear. Hello, Jackie." Then he went back to his paper. (A very normal and husbandly thing to do.)

I know that when I come home late, and Irving is watching the news on television, he won't even fade me with a "Hello, dear." In fact he doesn't even acknowledge my presence until Chet has said good night to David, and David says, "Good night, Chet." Then he gives me a casual smile and a "Hello, dear."

Now I'm not knocking "Hello dears." They're very nice to hear. And a husband is a glorious thing to have around the house. But after seeing Dorothy and Tinker together, I wanted a little fanfare of my own. I wanted someone to bounce to the door to meet me, to cover my face with adoring kisses, to follow me around the apartment. And as much as Irving loves me, he just is not the prancing, following type.

I began thinking. Thinking about poodles. It got so I stopped and stared every time I saw a poodle. And the more I stared, the more my convictions grew. EVERY poodle stared at its master with a look of complete idolatry. You've seen that look. The way a young painter looks at a Rembrandt or Titian. The way Liz Taylor looks at Richard Burton. The way Zsa Zsa looks at mink. That's how a poodle looks at its master.

I started staring in pet shop windows—but no longer as a spectator. Now I was a potential buyer. Let's face it! I was "hooked."

I still don't know how they do it. Perhaps it is mass hypnotism. Poodles do not believe atomic warfare will conquer the earth. Poodles believe, "The Cute Shall Inherit the Earth."

Suddenly I was "poodle shopping" in earnest. It isn't easy. After all, this isn't something you casually purchase like a Rolls Royce or a sable coat. Because this is something you have to live with. And note, I said *you* live with it, because it definitely does not live with you.

Also, I was well aware of a couple of very big obstacles.

Obstacle Number One

Poodles are not sold in Woolworth's like canaries. Poodles range in price from one hundred to six hundred dollars.

Solution

Give up my weekly massage. The massage cost ten bucks. In one year I would save five hundred and twenty dollars. This would not only cover the cost of the poodle, but would enable me to start a small annuity for the poodle's golden years. And my figure would not suffer due to the loss of the massage. The poodle would take care of that. After all, a poodle has to be exercised. Together we would share glorious nippy morning hikes in Central Park—climbing hills, the poodle dashing after pigeons and squirrels, me dashing after the poodle. It couldn't miss.

Obstacle Number Two

Irving.

Irving was not a dog lover. And if there was any dog Irving loved less than others, it was a poodle. He mentioned this fact every time he saw a poodle. And where we live there are more poodles than people.

Solution

None.

Play it by ear. Try prayer. Or faith. Or hysteria.

And so, in the month of March, in the year of 1954, I began my search to find some unsuspecting member of the Master Race to have, to hold, and to call me its very own.

3

The Search

The first step:	Learn everything about the breed.
The procedure:	Get chummy with a few poodle owners. They'll talk about the breed. (In fact, there's not very much else they do talk about.)
The hazards:	Avoid owners of other breeds.
Example:	A friend who owns a Yorkshire terrier will spend hours explaining why poodles are on the way out. A dachshund *aficionado* raves on and on about the brilliance and distinction of his breed. And then there's always the rugged individualist who gets on his knees and beseeches you to get the ONLY dog worth having. A boxer.

You sit and stare at the drooling object of his affection as he explains that a boxer is a "man's dog." And don't underrate the intelligence of this saliva-manufacturing monster. Because right in the middle of the pitch, he does his part to help cement the deal. With a surprise attack, he leaps on your lap and bestows a dripping suction pump of a kiss on your face. The best you can do is meekly extricate your nose and mouth from his mushy jaws and heartily agree on the imbecile's charm. Have you got a choice? He's twice your size!

All you can do is put on an act! Make all kinds of

sincere promises to think it over and inch toward the nearest exit. Pat the bruiser's head, slip out the door— and run for your life!

But even if you play it safe and stick to poodle owners, the going can get pretty rough.

You get *too much* advice. Everyone is an expert. Everyone knows about the *only* poodle farm in Westchester, Darien, or upstate New York. And everyone's poodle is a purebred marvel, with certified papers that prove he was sired by Champion Petite Cherie. The very same Champion Petite Cherie who won "Best of Show" in England, France, and West Berlin.

If these credentials are based on fact, this Champion Petite Cherie not only makes King Farouk sound like a regular homebody, but is also endowed with the dash and charm of the late Errol Flynn and the hormones of Charlie Chaplin.

Of course, if you're smart, you listen to no one. You form a mental picture of the kind of poodle you want and go out and get it. I listened to everyone. I also studied every size, shape, and color.

This is best accomplished on Fifth Avenue where it's not at all uncommon to see *one* woman sporting *three* poodles, all branching out from the same imported Italian leather leash. (Everything is Italian today, except the poodles.)

I reached my decision through a process of elimination.

A standard or substandard was too large. It would definitely crowd our double bed.

Toys can be adorable. Remember Wilbur, the champion white toy who took "Best of Show" at Madison Square Garden? But, unfortunately, all toys do not look like Wilbur. Or at least none of the toys I spotted prancing along the avenue. The young ones looked like thyroid cases. And the old ones looked like Peter Lorre. So it narrowed down to a miniature. The choice of color came next.

I made an instant decision the moment I met Tallulah. She was sitting in the bellboy's lap in our hotel lobby, licking his hand as he gently rubbed her ear. Tallulah was snow white, with a black beard and one black ear. This was for me! Distinctive, without being gaudy.

I asked the bellboy to find out where Tallulah was purchased.

He looked at me with open disapproval. "Mrs. Mansfield, Tallulah is a nice dog and all that. But you wouldn't want her. *She's a pari.*"

I didn't know what "pari" meant, but his tone implied it was definitely a social disease. And it is a social disease. Snobbery!

Do you know there is segregation among poodles?

Personally, I think it's outrageous, but who am I to fight the American Kennel Club? (The American Kennel Club will not allow a pari-colored poodle to be registered or shown at a dog show.) A poodle has to be all black, all white, all brown, all gray, all cocoa, all apricot—all anything as long as it's one color.

Originally, I suppose, poodles must have started out being white, black, and maybe brown. Three simple basic colors. (After all, did a mink ever dream that some day he'd be lavender?)

And poodles must have felt the same way. They were just sitting around being white, black, and brown until some breeder with a wild imagination decided to change all this. He mated a black one with a white. *Voila!* Gray children. Then he mated the gray with the white—you guessed it. Silver gray! A brown and white produced cocoa. Of course somewhere along the way, a white darling with a brown ear had to pop up. But it was worth it, because his brother and sister were pure apricot. However the white and brown misfit had to be sacrificed. Oh, I don't mean he was drowned at birth or left somewhere in the middle of the desert. Nothing as simple as that. After all, his owner could still get a fee for him, so he was sold as a household pet but barred for life from membership in the American Kennel Club. And do you know how neurotic this can make a poodle? Even if his master keeps this social stigma hidden from him, some loud-mouthed poodle he meets in the park will soon give him the facts of life.

Of course, there is a band of crusaders who meet underground to hold indignation meetings. They even send their congressmen signed petitions asking for equality for the pari. But at the present writing, integration has made no headway with the American Kennel Club.

Added to everything, a pari is very hard to find. Pet shops rarely display them.

Well, that eliminated the pari-colored darlings.

Black was the one color I didn't want. And white is too hard to keep clean. I got no "message" when I viewed the browns. Besides, if I was going to have a poodle, I decided I might as well go all out and get one of the jazzy shades. Apricot, silver, beige, or even fuchsia.

I made my final decision when I met Dipper. He was sleek, stunning, and silver. Edythe Kutlow, his owner, said Dipper's mother was going to have some new children in about seven months, and if I liked, I could put my name on the waiting list. But I am the impetuous type. I was not about to become a name on a list, sitting around waiting for a poodle to be born. I knew that somewhere, at that very moment, there was a poodle just sitting around, waiting to be discovered by me. And I was going to find him!

Of course, it had to be a "him." It was going to be rough enough to get Irving to live with *one* poodle. So it had to be a bachelor-type male, who would grow up to be a son and pal to Irving. Not a girl poodle who would transform him into a grandfather year after year.

4

The Poodle and Me

AFTER seeing Dipper and making my decision on color and size, I thought the rest would be easy. All I had to do was waltz out with a check in one hand and come back with a poodle in the other.

But it isn't that simple. Poodles shown in pet shops are for "tourists." If you're "hip" you get your poodle from a poodle breeder who has a poodle farm.

So I got out my little list. I went to the phone and began alphabetically. My first candidate was a Mrs. Addison in Westchester. I told Mrs. Addison I would drive out that afternoon and would she please have a few darling gray male poodles all gussied up for me to see.

Mrs. Addison said, "One minute, please."

Before I could interview the poodle, it seems Mrs. Addison wanted to interview me. Nothing personal. Just little routine questions. Like, just *which* Mrs. Mansfield was I? *Who* had recommended me? What was my religious faith? How did I feel about Senator Barry Goldwater?

I seemed to be getting by until she asked me if I intended to show the poodle.

I said of course I would show the poodle to all of my friends. After all, I didn't intend to hide it in the closet.

This got Mrs. Addison a little edgy. In a patronizing tone she said, "I mean, is the poodle going to *appear* in shows?"

I was flattered as I realized Mrs. Addison had probably seen me on television and was a fan. But why does everyone want to get into the act? I felt it was up to me to decide whether or not *my* poodle had theatrical inclinations. So I said maybe the poodle would appear with me from time to time, but I wasn't prepared to arrive and hand him a signed contract.

Mrs. Addison said she was not alluding to television shows. And then she came up with that immortal line: "Mr. Addison and I wouldn't *have* a television set in the house. Even our children think it's a time waster and a bore."

Then this endearing woman went on to explain that the shows she spoke of were sporting events. Dog shows.

I was delighted to say that the nearest I had ever gotten to a dog show was when Lassie appeared on television and that I intended to keep it that way.

I could feel Mrs. Addison getting giant hives right over the phone. Her voice had a gurgly sound as she choked back her anger. "If you don't intend to show the dog, then why do you want a poodle from the Addison Farm?"

When I said, "Just for a pet," Mrs. Addison didn't answer.

Mrs. Addison had hung up.

Well . . . back to the drawing board.

I went through all the A's and B's on my list with much the same results. And when I got to the C's, a Miss Cosgrove as much as told me to go out and buy a canary if I merely wanted a household pet.

I was almost a basket case when I got to Mr. Zussman. His poodles had to be "shown" too. But he was a very kind man and even admitted he owned a television set. And he tried to explain that it was fun to show a dog. And so simple. I listened. What else could I do? He was the last name on my list.

It seems first you register the dog with the American Kennel Club. (No matter how you slice it, that name always crops up.) But you must send in a choice of several names to the American Kennel Club. Because if some other dog has the name you have chosen, you can't have it.

(Well, I went along with that. Actor's Equity and AFTRA have the same rules.)

Obedience School came next, Mr. Zussman explained. The dog had to learn how to walk.

(All those dogs you see walking gaily down the street only *think* they're walking. They're slobs compared to a dog who has been taught to walk.)

The tail has to be held at a certain angle. The head a certain way. There are several paces to be learned —a walk, a trot—it's usually a six-month's course.

I found myself going along with it, even fading Mr. Zussman with an occasional "you don't say," or "how interesting." After all, it didn't sound much different from those ads taken by the charm schools. So I'd have a high-fashion-type poodle.

Then Mr. Zussman came up with the blockbuster. "Of course, you have to attend classes with the dog."

Now I didn't expect the dog to walk to school carrying his own books, but on the other hand, I didn't think I'd have to sit through classes with him. Didn't they have some kind of a bus service like all fancy nursery schools?

Mr. Zussman said, "But they have to teach *you* how to walk."

That did it!

I told Mr. Zussman that my walk might not be any challenge to Brigitte Bardot, but I had managed to appear in several Broadway shows without falling over the furniture. And even though I did *sit* on panels on TV shows, I assured him that there were times when I *walked* on and off.

But as I said, Mr. Zussman was a patient man. He explained I had to learn to use a different walk in the show ring.

In other words, the dog doesn't do a "single" when

it goes on. It's the star, but you're right there, trotting around at the other end of the leash, playing a supporting role.

And as Mr. Zussman pointed out, how would it look if the dog walked like a duchess but didn't win because it had a slob on the other end of the leash. Of course, if I weren't up to it I could always hire a handler.

Well, don't challenge me. I had walked my way through the early Milton Berle show right down to glorious living tape, and a thing like a dog ring wasn't going to throw me.

I'd take things as they came. Meanwhile, first things first. So I told Mr. Zussman I'd drive up the following day. Then as an afterthought I added, "And be sure to have one with the mustache and beard. I hate those clean-cut faces."

I should have quit when I was ahead.

This time it was Mr. Zussman who faltered. "A mustache and beard? Are you thinking of the Dutch Clip?"

I said I sure was—with the padded shoulders and padded rear.

Mr. Zussman said, "Forget it."

"Forget what?"

"The Dutch Clip. A show dog can't have anything but a 'Show Clip.'"

I asked what was a Show Clip.

Mr. Zussman explained.

I wish I had never asked.

I had seen a Show Clip on a few neurotic, mortified poodles. The ones that cause you to stop, stare, and say, "Good God! What is *that?*" The head has a massive lion mane, out of which peeks a bare and miserable little face. The body from the waist down is totally without fur, and ridiculous little pompons adorn the legs and tail.

And so as the sun set on the beautiful hills of New York's skyscrapers, I took my leave of Mr. Zussman on the telephone.

I wasn't discouraged. I was hysterical.

I called all those "friends" who had given me the names on this list and demanded to know how come they walked around with poodles that sported a Dutch Clip if they had patronized these farms.

Naturally I got all kinds of alibis. Some said they hadn't *actually* gotten their poodle from the farm itself; it was the *son* of a poodle from that farm. A few said they had gone all through the Obedience bit and shown the dogs. They even had certificates to prove their dogs were bona fide champions. But there was no rule stating the dog couldn't retire once the championship was won. Then he could even let his hair grow back and walk around like a civilian-type poodle.

It looked as though I had no alternative but to sit around and wait until Edythe Kutlow's contact had another romance.

Except that Joyce Mathews (Mrs. Billy Rose) chose this moment to return from Europe. And Joyce had a poodle. Billy had given it to her the previous year. At that time I had not been "poodle-struck," so I had merely given the little ball of fluff a loving pat and watched it trundle out of the room.

Joyce's arrival, I decided, had been timed by fate. Her poodle must be full-grown by now. She would have all the answers. And not once could I recall ever hearing her mention that either she or Billy had attended any Obedience classes.

And if Joyce had a poodle, it had to be a good poodle. After all, everyone knows that Billy Rose is the type of man who surrounds himself with the best of everything. He has the biggest town house in New York City. When he wants sun in the winter, he doesn't fool around with Florida. He bought himself a hunk of the British West Indies. And when it comes to country estates in the summer, he doesn't have just an estate. He went out and bought himself a whole island.

And everyone knows about Billy's taste. When you

see a Van Gogh on a wall in one of Billy's homes, you
know this is not a sixty-nine-cent copy. And if you
find a scratch on the Henry the Eighth silver, it's there
because Henry was a slob—not Billy.

When he drives from house to house, it's in a Rolls
Royce.

When he got married, it was to Joyce Mathews, one
of the most beautiful girls in the world. And he even
did this in big style. He married Joyce twice (at the
present writing).

This was it! Who would be more qualified to give
me poodle advice? Would a man like Billy inject an
inferior poodle into such a superior setup?

Also, Billy is not the type of man who would take
any loyalty oaths before buying a poodle. I'd put him
up against Mrs. Addison and her group any day.

I called Joyce immediately. She listened quietly as
I explained about the woman in Westchester. Oddly
enough Joyce knew all about her. She said the Westchester lady was a living doll. It was the lady in Wil-
ton who was the real killer. And not even to attempt
Mrs. Dodge-Higgens in Rye.

She had gone through the whole agonizing treatment. That's why she had turned the matter over to
Billy. After all, when Billy ran night clubs in the
twenties, it was often necessary for him to have personal contact with some of those famous men whose
life stories appear on "The Untouchables." And Billy
had come through all in one piece. And lest you think
Billy is all brawn, I must remind you that Billy is also
equally at home in the Parke-Bernet Galleries.

This, too, is another plus for "poodle shopping."
And Billy hadn't let her down. Within one hour after
receiving the "contract," Billy came home with a
poodle.

His great secret? He just marched into a pet store
and bought one.

He didn't need Mrs. Addison's advice or detailed instructions from the A.K.C. After all, a producer who

has dreamed up the Aquacade and redecorated theaters, homes, and islands is equipped with the eye of an artist. He can recognize a fine poodle when he sees one. I asked whether Billy would go to the same pet shop and help me select a poodle.

She said, "Of course, if you really want him to." There was something missing from her voice. Like enthusiasm.

I said I wanted to see this selection of Billy's now that it was full-grown. She said to come right over. She and the selection were spending the day at home.

Joyce was in her bedroom, unpacking her trunks, when I arrived. But there was no sign of the selection. Joyce told the maid to bring him in.

The maid froze. "Me?"

Joyce nodded. The maid went off with a worried look. I asked what she had named him. She said she hadn't gotten around to it yet.

"But you've had him close to a year!"

Joyce said, "A name has to 'go' with a dog. Maybe you can come up with something. I can't."

Then the maid entered, dragging in something resembling a crocodile. It leaped nimbly on the bed, smashing only a small lamp and the night table.

"He's grown, hasn't he?" I said politely.

Joyce nodded. His papers stated that he was a purebred miniature. But this dog had a mind of his own, and he had decided to grow. God, how he had grown! In sections! He had the head of a standard, the body of a substandard, and the legs of a dachshund. Also, he must have been so busy growing that he forgot to take time out to grow any fur. His body sported a few motheaten wisps of hair that might have looked stunning on an Airedale—but on a poodle it looked kind of offbeat.

"Billy refuses to admit he made a mistake," Joyce explained. "He says this is just an adolescent period and that suddenly one day he'll be a beautiful poodle." (Her voice lacked a certain inner conviction.)

"He has nice eyes." (I had to say something. The dog was staring at me.)

"What would *you* name him?" Joyce asked. "Maybe Fluffy? Or Cuddles?"

With a horrified expression, the dog dived under the bed. I suggested we try to think of a good rugged French name. Maybe the name of some great hero in French literature would suit him. Naturally, she came up with "Quasimodo."

I said I thought he looked more like Toulouse Lautrec. After all, his eyes were very much like José Ferrer's.

I could tell from Joyce's expression I had hit pay dirt. "Toulouse." She cooed the name. Then she scrambled on the floor. "Toulouse, where are you? You've got a name."

The namesake was all snug and comfy under the bed, dining on one of my kid gloves. I went to retrieve it and was rewarded with a snarl.

"Don't worry about it," she insisted. "It won't hurt him. He has a cast-iron stomach."

This last statement was made not without some maternal pride. "And he hasn't had any childhood ailments like most poodles," she went on. "When he broke his leg, the big plaster cast didn't hinder him at all. He was still able to wreck a whole room of furniture."

I realized that grotesque as he was, he was *hers*, and she cared for him. This bantering about his looks was just a façade. She *wanted* to believe that he'd be like other poodles some day. So, like any good friend, I lied outrageously and said he really was quite attractive when you got to know him. In fact, he had a rakish charm and was really quite stunning up close.

I could see I had gone too far.

Joyce just stared at me. Then she poured out her pent-up feelings. Of course she loved him, but oh, the humiliations she had suffered. Each time she took him for a walk it was always the same. People stared, then gave her a glazed look, followed with, "What *is* it?"

Headwaiters and captains had also been cruel. Take "21" for example. In the luxurious living room that serves as a waiting room, it is not uncommon to find five or six fancy beribboned poodles tied to chairs, waiting for their owners who are dining inside. Naturally, Joyce brought her specimen there one day. She was greeted with the familiar gasp, the eternal "What *is* it?" followed with the routine glazed look. But at "21" the look was topped off with a disdainful stare.

Joyce returned the stare with a bravado she did not feel, and the captain backed down. He had no recourse but to accept the object gingerly and tie him to a chair, just as if he were a regular French poodle.

But Joyce is familiar with caste system—like the right and wrong side of El Morocco. And there was nothing she could do as she watched the captain haughtily tie her darling to a chair in the *back* of the room, not up front where the elegant poodles sat. And there had been several front chairs vacant.

I felt such sympathy for both Joyce and Toulouse that I reacted as any devoted friend would react. I rubbed his head and gave him my other glove for dessert. But we hadn't solved my problem. I was still without a poodle.

Joyce suggested I go to a pet store and buy one that was a year old. That would be playing it safe—it would be full-grown, and I would know what I was getting.

I dismissed this idea immediately. Everyone knows that when you adopt a child the best course is to take him when he is five or six days old. Then it is really *your* child. In fact, it often grows up to look like you, your husband, or your rich Aunt Emma.

Of course, you are taking a risk. *Every* baby starts out with a button nose and no teeth. So what if it grows a nose like Cyrano? There *are* plastic surgeons. And if the teeth start looking like piano keys, there *are* braces and caps. Today *everyone* can be beautiful. Even your own flesh and blood baby can sprout some features that belong to an ugly cousin on your husband's side. Everyone takes a chance with babies. Because, unfortunately, the little darlings do grow up to be people. But you still don't sit around and wait for a baby to be twenty-five or thirty years old before you adopt him.

I felt it was the same with a poodle. I had to take my chances. Not that I expected it to look like Irving or me. At this point I was just rooting it would look like a poodle.

I decided it would do no harm just to browse around in a pet shop. Naturally, after seeing Toulouse, I had no intention of making any snap judgment purchase. I might even wind up doing the Obedience Training School and Westchester bit. At least I'd wind up with a poodle that would get a front chair at "21."

Since I was "just looking," I wandered into the first pet shop I saw. It has long since gone out of business, but on that day its windows were chock full of poodle puppies.

At the age of three months no poodle looks like a poodle. They are all adorable balls of fluff. And they all act as if they firmly intend to grow up to be beautiful poodles. But clinging to the mental image of Toulouse, I refused to allow these balls of fluff to hypnotize me. I told the owner I was just looking and would especially like to look at some gray male miniatures. He placed several black balls on the floor before me.

I reminded him that I had asked for silver gray. In answer, he parted their fur, and amazingly enough, there was an inch of silver fur growing in at the roots. Like a blonde needing a touchup—in reverse. He explained that all "silvers" are born black.

I liked them all, but I didn't seem to get any message from any of them. (Somehow, I had expected I would get a special feeling when the right poodle came along.

You know—that mysterious communication we'd both feel the moment our eyes met.)

I explained this to the owner of the store. He said he handled hundreds of poodles, and he had never gotten one message. And he looked into their eyes every day. It didn't happen that way. You picked a poodle for its lines and pedigree, and after you lived together, *then* you get the message.

He showed me their papers. Very impressive. But reminding myself that Toulouse also had impressive papers, I began to think of a good exit line. I inched toward the wall that was lined with cages and said they were all darling, but I would have to go home and sleep on it.

He held up one in particular and began to brush its fur. I said it was glorious but I'd have to think it over. He warned me it might be gone the following day.

Suddenly something reached out of a cage and touched my shoulder. I turned around and the small paw came out again and playfully tapped me. I asked the owner what it was. He said it was a poodle. I asked him to take it out and show it to me.

He said that would be silly as it was everything I didn't want. It was a true black. Its mother had been a miniature, but its father had been a toy. So it would be smaller than the average miniature and too large to be classed as a toy. It was also a female. Silly even to look at it. He began to brush the dog he was holding and, with recharged energy, pointed out its excellent points.

I asked him to take the "everything-I-didn't want" one out of its cage. He ignored me and quoted a new and more favorable price on the dog he was holding. In return, I pointed back to the cage on the wall. With a shrug, he opened the cage, saying it was a waste of time—I'd never select this dog.

I said it seemed to have selected me.

He placed it on the floor with the other dogs who were twice its size. IT immediately pranced over and snatched away a toy with which they were playing. The three "gray" dogs advanced menacingly. IT stood its ground, and with the toy in its mouth, held up a paw defiantly. The three larger dogs backed away.

Then IT turned and looked at me for approval and dropped the toy at my feet. I picked IT up and IT began to kiss my cheek with a rough little tongue.

The owner said it was really too young to tell how it would turn out. It was only eight weeks old. It could grow into a misshapen hulk. A technicolor vision of Toulouse shot through my mind.

This man was giving me facts, I warned myself. A ball of fluff *does* grow. I mustn't let the charm of a few pink-tongued kisses go to my head. I didn't want a black poodle. I couldn't get stuck with a female. I thought it all out carefully, then said, "I'll take this dog."

Suddenly his whole personality changed. He became uneasy. He said he was expecting some new beautiful silver grays at the end of the week. Why not come back then? He reached for the small black bundle of fur in my arms. I pulled back. She gave me a sideswipe of a kiss as a reward. I asked the price.

He came up with something that sounded like a year's rent. I told him that was an outrageous figure. He agreed and reached for the dog. I held on. She gave me another quick kiss. We stood staring in deadlock.

He said, "Look, lady, there's no price tag on her neck. I didn't force her on you. You either pay the price or put her back in the cage."

I said, "But this is an outrageous price for a female miniature."

He agreed it was. Then the truth came out. He didn't really want to sell her. She came from a bloodline that threw off magnificent coats. He wanted to keep her and breed her. Her puppies would bring a very high price. Especially if she were bred with a toy. Then her puppies would be true toys, with great coats.

I stared at the small baby in my arms who was being sentenced to the life of a bordello queen, doomed to turn out assembly-line children for this horrible ped-dler of flesh and fur. I had to save this innocent angel.

I started to haggle like an outraged Frenchwoman at the flea market. The owner haggled right back. Dogs began to bark; people began to stare. But I had no choice. I didn't have the price, and I was determined that this little angel was not going to be put into white slavery.

The owner came down fifty dollars. After all, even the canaries were beginning to scream. But he was still twenty-five dollars over my top price. I stood my ground and argued.

He said he had a right to ask any price he wanted to for an animal with such a magnificent coat. With that, he tried to yank her from my arms. The "magnificent coat" sank two sharp baby teeth right into his fingers. He took off the final twenty-five dollars and said he hoped he'd never see either of us again.

I gave him a check, put her under my coat, and dashed into a cab and brought her home. I had found my poodle. Of course, deep down, I knew it was the other way around. That poodle had sat in that cage for a week or more just casing parents. She had found me!

5

And Daddy Makes Three

THE PANIC didn't set in until I got home and deposited my prize in the middle of the living room. It was then that some small voice within me suddenly shrieked, "Now what?"

"Now what?" was right! I had just ended a beautiful friendship with the Chase Manhattan Bank in exchange for three exquisite pounds of poodle. I knew I would not regret it because I was madly in love with the poodle And I also knew the poodle was madly in love with me. But that's all I knew.

Since the pet shop proprietor and I had not exactly parted with a long and tender farewell, it suddenly hit me that I had left without learning some important facts. Like what to feed the little darling. And when?

And then there was Irving! He was still unaware of the thrill that was awaiting him. How *would* Irving react? Unfortunately, I have a vivid imagination. I *knew* how Irving would react. I took a Miltown.

Then I decided to call the owner of the pet shop. Let him scream. I'd scream right back. It would be a good warmup exercise for my session with Irving. It started out better than I expected. His assistant answered the phone. He was glad I had called. He wanted my address.

I asked why? (After all, this *is* New York City. You have to be careful.)

He said, "Don't you want her papers? And the

American Kennel Club form? You want to register her, don't you?"

I said I really didn't care one way or another.

"But you can't get a decent male to sire her puppies without papers or an A.K.C. registration!"

Puppies! And she still didn't have all her baby teeth. I was sure glad I had rescued her. This pet shop was run by a couple of sex degenerates.

Then his voice took on a pleading tone. "Lady, when you *do* mate her, let us have first crack at her puppies. Oh, and *please* consult us about the male. We'll be glad to arrange stud service."

I said that before all this future action took place, we should show some concern for the present. Like tomorrow's breakfast. What was this siren supposed to eat?

He said, "Chopped meat mixed with canned evaporated milk."

"For breakfast?"

"For breakfast, lunch, tea time, and dinner. Four times a day."

Well, all I could do was give it a whirl. But first things first. Daddy was coming home shortly. And she had to make a good impression.

The right setting was important. After all, doesn't Tiffany's sometimes place just one diamond in a window encased with black velvet? I tried my little gem on the living room couch. Not right—they were both black. It had to be the bedroom. The white moire bedspread was a marvelous backdrop. I placed her on the middle of the bed. She stretched out and rolled on her back like a little princess. She *was* a little princess. A little French princess. I immediately named her Josephine. She immediately relieved herself on the moire bedspread.

I told myself not to panic. After all, we had a marvelous cleaner. He'd make it look just like new. Meanwhile, I quickly tore it off and hid it in the closet.

We returned to the living room. I sat down on the red club chair and held her on my lap. Not as effective as the white moire—but a fairly striking setting. Ten minutes later, I changed my dress and began to feel some concern about the state of her kidneys.

An hour later the appearance of the apartment had undergone a radical transformation. Newspapers covered every inch of the rug. Every chewable object like bedroom slippers, telephone cords, throw pillows had been removed from the floor. And in the middle of this we sat—waiting for Irving to come home and face all this gloriousness.

Of all days, Irving chose this day to be late. And from the way things were going, I was beginning to wonder if Josephine would live long enough to meet him.

This dog had a fetish about "togetherness." If I sat on a chair in the living room, she immediately nestled on my foot and fell into instant sleep. Two minutes later the phone would ring. I'd go to answer it. Josie would wake up, follow me, taking only a short detour to relieve herself on the one spot of the rug that wasn't covered with newspaper. Then she promptly settled on my foot to resume her nap. I'd hang up, apologetically arouse Josie, and dash to clean the spot on the rug. She co-operated by scampering off with the sponge, upsetting the bowl of water, and playing tug of war with my skirt. Then as I scurried back to the kitchen for some rags to mop up the cleaning water, I found that Josie, for the first time, had left my side. I broke all track records getting back to the bedroom, arriving just in time to see Josephine polish off the final piece of soap as if it were Baked Alaska. There was no sign of the sponge, but from the fragments on her whiskers, I could see that it had been the appetizer.

Eventually we returned to the chair in the living room and she once more demonstrated her second biggest talent—instant sleep. The phone rang, but I refused to answer it, and things were quite peaceful for about ten minutes, until she suddenly decided to throw up the soap. She also threw in the sponge!

When we finally returned to the living room chair, it was a tossup as to which one of us fell asleep first, but the next thing I heard was the sound of Irving's key in the lock.

I could tell he had had a good day. He was whistling. I sat rigid. Josie was more daring. She got off my shoe and wandered out to the foyer to investigate. Irving stopped whistling. Slowly he entered the room.

In a weak voice I said, "Josie, this is Daddy."

She got the idea immediately. She rushed to him with such force that she toppled over. Irving seemed to have turned to bronze. Josie tried a little more charm. In fact she threw in her whole bag of tricks. She chewed at his shoelaces. She rolled over on her back. She played cops and robbers with his trousers. She even forced herself to make another puddle on the newspaper.

Irving finally regained his power of speech. He said, "What is it? And whom does it belong to?" (Now I ask you, did he think every French poodle went around calling him "Daddy"?)

I fluttered my eyelashes, and dripping more charm than a king-sized Arlene Francis, cooed, "It's *ours*, darling."

He said, "Get rid of it immediately." Then he stalked into the bedroom.

Well, I hadn't expected it to be easy. I fixed a nice long Scotch, just the way he liked it, and brought it into the bedroom. Then I went into a dramatic plea of how a poodle could only add to our happiness. Think of the joys of sharing our abode with a living, breathing pet, whose only point in living was to bathe us in undying love and affection.

He said it might come as a shock to me, but the last thing he wanted to bathe in was a poodle's affection. I gave him my cheeriest grin. (You see, I'd read Arlene's book on charm. Arlene claims charm can move mountains.) But it wasn't moving Irving.

So after ten minutes of absolute failure, I gave up the charm and acted naturally. I had hysterics. I wouldn't say I was successful, but at least I got his attention. He had to spend the next ten minutes calming me and reassuring me of his love. Of course he wouldn't throw a defenseless puppy out on the street tonight. But tomorrow he'd give it to Florence Lustig for her darling little boy. The puppy would have a good home and I could visit it whenever I wished. He lit a cigarette for me. As far as he was concerned, the crisis was over and the matter had been settled. He blissfully returned to his paper and drink. But he couldn't enjoy himself. I was silent. I was also staring at him.

He put down the paper, and in a "this-is-it-I-have-spoken" voice said, "Look, Jackie, she *is* going! No amount of tears will change my mind." He stared at me defiantly. I glared back. But I knew he was right. This was no time for tears. This time I fainted.

6

On Trial

NATURALLY, I won a reprieve. Irving had sold a new television show that was to emanate from the Coast during the summer. We were leaving for California the end of June. I could keep Josephine until then. Then, I was to present her as a permanent gift to Florence Lustig for her son, Craig.

I had to give Irving an agreement in writing that not even a small trauma would occur when this separation took place. I signed it willingly. After all, this gave me three months. In three months anything could happen. Maybe the show would be canceled.

Of course I didn't voice such a thought. "Canceled" is an obscene word along Madison Avenue. It's comparable to a news flash that Russian tanks are crossing the George Washington Bridge.

I also had to agree to certain absolute rules:

1. He would never walk her—or even accompany me when I walked her. (If I wanted to make a spectacle of myself with that ridiculous object at the end of a leash, that was up to me.)

2. He would never never clean up a puddle.

3. All expenses incurred by her were to come out of my own pocket. (Unless, of course, she met with a quick and sudden death. Then he would spring for one hell of a funeral.)

4. At all times she was to stay out of his way!

We shook hands on these rules, and on this happy note Josephine's family life with the Mansfields began.

Irving's lack of parental affection in no way damp-
ened her spirit or charm. She grew more adorable day
by day. The first day she learned to bark at every
sound in the hall. She also barked all night. The second
day she learned how to jump on the bed and wake
Daddy at dawn with adorable wet kisses. The third
day she learned to eat the plaster off the wall. The
fourth day she learned how to have a convulsion.

Irving said it must have been something she ate.
Like adhesive tape, his golf socks, a plastic bottle top,
or those imported French sequins from an evening
bag I was sure had been put out of her reach. A hurried consultation with the pet shop owner brought
me the assurance that frequent dosages of a mild laxative would restore order within twenty-four hours.

Naturally, this new development, coupled with her
athletic kidneys, necessitated a temporary confinement
of living quarters. As for the mild laxative, I selected
Fletcher's Castoria. (After all, the ads say, "Children
Cry for It!") I turned the kitchen over to her as a
boudoir. It was a typical hotel kitchen—a closet, fur-
nished with a sink and refrigerator. I generously lined
the kitchen with newspaper, placed her in it, sur-
rounded her with all the luxuries of home. Her bed,
water, toys, and yummies. Then I poured some of the
Fletcher's Castoria down her throat and told her that
as soon as things got back to normal she could have
the run of the place. I kissed her good night and closed
the kitchen door.

Josephine immediately came up with another hidden
talent. This girl was gifted with a pair of pipes that
could put Maria Callas out of the business. I opened
the door and the aria stopped. It was immediately replaced with ecstatic tail thumping and smiling bliss.
I figured maybe the Fletcher's Castoria had already
done the trick. She gratefully trotted into the living
room while I surveyed the kitchen. Nothing. *The
New York Times* was in perfect condition. I stared
at her as she chased a ball in the living room. She

seemed to feel fine. And five minutes later she felt even better when she threw up the Fletcher's Castoria.

I gave her another shot of the Castoria and put her back in the kitchen. I explained it wasn't forever. Tomorrow we'd pack in the Castoria and go visit a doctor. But for tonight, she had to stay in the kitchen. She seemed to get the idea and agreeably settled in her little wicker bed. I could see she was a reasonable dog.

Until I closed the door. Then back came the operatic solo. She hit notes above high C that haven't even been invented. I rushed to the book I had just purchased. The author presumably runs several kennels. I sat and read it from cover to cover while Josephine went through an entire repertoire by Puccini. The author states, "Be firm . . . use a strong hand if necessary. Don't be afraid to whip the dog. He'll respect you. He wants to feel you are his superior . . . his master. Above all . . . remember at all times . . . you are *his* master. If he eats something wrong, smack his mouth . . . if he refuses to be housebroken or to obey, smack his rear." Several times I had to look back at the cover to reassure myself it was a book on the love and care of a dog and not the memoirs of Adolph Eichmann.

The owner of the pet shop, who was now getting to be like a blood relative, had suggested putting an alarm clock beside her. Puppies don't like to be alone. But if they hear the loud tick of an alarm clock, they will think someone is with them. That's what the owner of the pet shop said. Josie had three alarm clocks around her, but obviously she was smarter than the owner of the pet shop. She knew the difference between clocks and people.

At two o'clock in the morning she was still in perfect voice. Irving asked me whether I intended to do something about it. Of course, I ignored him. At three o'clock in the morning the manager of the hotel phoned and told me I had better do something about it. I couldn't ignore him. I was in a dilemma. I told

Irving I had two alternatives. Let her sleep with us (which was her original idea) or I could go in the kitchen and sleep with her. Irving immediately solved my problem by eliminating one of the alternatives. I set up camp in the kitchen. She stopped vocalizing the moment I joined her and slept right through the night. I know, because I sat there and watched her. In the morning, the bellboys at our hotel directed me to a very good vet. (Bellboys know everything.)

I shall call this establishment Dr. White's Dog and Cat Hospital, and if there is any Dr. White either living or dead, it is purely coincidental. After all, why should Josephine give up all her royalties on this book just to pay off Louis Nizer?

Of course, I didn't get to see Dr. White himself. HE was in surgery. I was turned over to Dr. Black, a member of his staff. He examined Josephine's throat and scowled. He looked in her ears and frowned. I asked if anything was wrong.

He said, "Keep quiet until the examination is over." (Sure, I had to find the Ben Casey of the vets.)

Finally, the examination was completed to his satisfaction. He said, "How long have you had this dog?"

I told him we were currently celebrating our sixth day together.

He glowered. "Where did you get her?"

I told him the name of the pet shop.

"Take her back!" It was a command.

Take her back?

He scowled. "This pup was weaned too early. She has a virus through her entire system. She's had it for about two weeks. Sometimes you can lick it if you catch it right away, but she's too far gone. Return the dog and get your money back—or another dog. If they won't do it, call me. I'll report them to the A.K.C. They sold you a dying dog."

Then he yelled for his assistant to get me some smelling salts. When my strength returned, I began to scream. I didn't want my money back. I didn't want another dog. This was the only dog for me. Why, she was my flesh and fur. He *had* to save her.

Josie got the idea something was up and co-operated magnificently. She began to screech and vomit simultaneously. Dogs who were confined to cages in other parts of the hospital also raised their voices in sympathy. Several customers who were waiting in the outer office immediately grabbed their dogs and made a hasty exit.

The doctor finally agreed to take her as a patient. He held out very little hope. (In fact, at that moment, I think his only hope was to get me out of the building.) He also warned me there was going to be great expense involved in her treatment.

Money! At a time like this! From the disdainful look I gave him, you might have thought I was Paul Getty's only living heir. But expense was not the only factor involved. There were rules to be adhered to:

1. She was to remain at the hospital for a week.

2. During that week, under no circumstances was I to set foot in the hospital.

3. I was to phone only once a day, and no matter what news I received on the phone, I was not to tie up the switchboard with threats or hysterics of any kind.

With that, he rang the buzzer. An attendant whisked Josephine into the X-ray room, and I was shown the door.

The week that followed was the longest week of my life. But for Irving, the days just flew. It was nothing personal against Josephine, he explained. He certainly wished her a speedy recovery and all that, but it was thrilling to walk on carpets instead of the *Times*. Each day I called the hospital. I would like to meet that sadist in the medical profession who invented the following phrases: "Patient's condition unchanged." "Patient is holding his own." "Patient seemed to have a restful night."

I don't know which is worse, those "tell nothing" phrases or the one that greeted me on the seventh day. "The doctor would like to see you." That's all. No explanation. As thrilling and personal as the Bell Telephone's weather recording.

Irving caught me as I charged out of the apartment. He forced me to sit down for a small heart to heart. It was obvious he got the same inference of "the doctor would like to see you" line.

He opened with, "Now, Jackie—" (This always means "please be reasonable.")

"Now, Jackie, I want you to promise me something."

I nodded dumbly. I was anxious to get to the hospital. In his best soothing-type voice he explained that if the doctor wanted to "put her to sleep," I was not to go into a trauma, threaten his life, or go berserk. I was to remember that this doctor had not personally planned her illness as a plot against me. I must keep in mind that this doctor had gone to college, studied, and gotten a degree because he loved animals and wanted to keep them healthy and alive. I was to accept whatever council he offered, and above all, I was to bear in mind she was only a dog. And as a dog she had enjoyed five action-packed, glorious days with us. Why, most dogs live an entire lifetime without knowing a second of such luxury and love. Then, as a final generous and thoughtful gesture, he handed me a signed blank check.

I stared at it. He was sweet. He wanted me to rush out and buy another dog. Never underestimate mental telepathy. With a wild look he added, "That check is for hospital expenses. She's probably run up quite a bill. And there'll also be an added fee if they want to put her to sleep. I know I told you that you had to carry all her expenses, but if she's got to go, I want her to go in style!"

7

Our Little
Do-It-Yourself Sanitarium

When I reached the hospital, there was no waiting around. I was rushed right into Dr. White's private office. Of course, there was no sign of Dr. White. He was in surgery. But my buddy, Dr. Black, was there. Nothing had changed. Not even his charming disposition. He got right to the point.

"Mrs. Mansfield, you know how sick the dog was when you brought her here. It was an impossible situation. She wouldn't eat for three days. We had to resort to 'force feeding.' " (I must be calm. At least she's still alive.)

"We even kept a doctor on night duty, just for her. We kept the virus under control with penicillin. But a dog cannot live without food and water." (Maybe she isn't alive.)

"We tried intravenous, but it didn't do much good. There is nothing we did not try." (She *was* dead.)

"That's why I sent for you, Mrs. Mansfield . . ." (I mustn't faint when they bring out the little casket.)

"We've done everything we could. As I said, the virus is under control. But she must have food and water. If she'll eat for anyone, perhaps she'll eat for you. That's why we suggest you take her home."

Take her home! He began to shout for help as I covered his adorable face with kisses. I gazed at him lovingly as he pried himself loose and began writing

prescriptions and feeding instructions. He warned me
not to let her fluffy coat deceive me. She was down to
skin and bones. I *had* to get some weight on her.

Then the attendant brought her in. She almost ex-
ploded with love and delight! She squealed, she kissed
me, she wagged her entire body with such gusto I
almost heard her ribs rattle. I guess I squealed and
gurgled, too. For once the doctor was patient as
Josephine and I went through an exceedingly dramatic reunion.

When we finally stopped kissing and squealing, I
took time out to fill in Irving's blank check and listen
to Dr. Black's final instructions. She was to return in
ten days for another distemper shot and a checkup.
She was not to set one dainty foot outdoors until May
—if she lived till May. If I didn't get some food down
her, she would be gone in forty-eight hours. I wasn't
worried about that. She would eat anything for me.
While I was holding her, listening to the doctor, she
had practically had a full course dinner, licking all
the make-up off my face.

When Irving came home that evening and saw the
News and *Mirror* covering the floor, he went into a
quiet state of shock. He didn't even share my enthusiasm when I told him Josie had eaten a whole lamb
chop and a dish of rice pudding. But he was curious
as to how I had suddenly mastered such culinary arts.
After all, it was still touch and go with me every
morning on the instant coffee.

I stared at him. Hadn't he ever heard of room service? For some strange reason this reminded him of
his signed blank check. He asked me to return it!
After all, when it came to funeral arrangements, he
had been more than willing to go all out. But never
once had he indicated he would sponsor her survival.
And in gourmet style!

Josephine inched toward him as he spoke and gently licked his hand. And when I said I had used the
check, she began licking in double time. (This dog

knew where her next room service meal was coming from.)

Of course, I fired back some pretty snappy retorts. Like "Haven't you any soul?" "Don't you think she's cute?"

He said, all right, she was cute. But what could she do for him? What was she going to contribute to our lives? She was just a living, breathing piece of nuisance value, especially designed to scream all night, rob him of a roommate, destroy his apartment, wearing apparel, and peace of mind. And at the rate she was going, she cost more to run than a Cadillac.

All through this tirade he unconsciously rubbed her head as she snuggled against his leg. When I pointed out this action, he was exasperated.

"What do you expect me to do? Hit her over the head with a baseball bat?" Then, as he stalked out of the room, he tossed as a clincher, "Shall I move your pillow and blanket into the kitchen now, or wait till tonight when she raises that glorious voice in song?"

But Josie had her own plans for the evening. She wasn't deceived by that phoney smile Irving threw at her whenever she caught his eye. She knew all about Florence Lustig and her little boy, Craig. She was also positive the virus bit was Irving's idea. Why, she had never felt a moment's discomfort.

But just because she had expressed a little vocal disapproval regarding her sleeping quarters, he had "banished" her off to a place where she had been stashed away in a cage, stuck with needles, and subjected to all kinds of indignities and humiliations. She was determined not to let that happen again.

She had it all figured out. "She loves me. He doesn't. Well, that's the way the cooky crumbles. So if she puts me in the kitchen, well let's face it, the kitchen is more comfortable than that cage I just left. And besides, no one will come along in the middle of the night and jab a needle in my derrière." That's the way she figured it. (But how was I to know?)

So when I put her in the kitchen, she merely licked my hand, gave me a knowing nod, climbed into her twenty-dollar wicker bed, and didn't even let out a small practice scale when I closed the door.

I got into bed beside Irving, put out the light and we both settled down and waited for the aria. Naturally, it didn't come. After five minutes, Irving yawned. "Thank God, she's decided to let us sleep." Ten minutes of too silent silence followed.

Finally I whispered, "Irving, are you still awake?"

IRVING: Well, I am now.

ME: What do you suppose she's doing in there?

IRVING: Maybe she's making a Spanish omelet. Who cares, as long as she keeps her mouth shut!

ME: But it's too quiet. Do you think I should take a peek?

IRVING: Look, I'm not especially on her side, but when she's right, she's right. The poor dog is just trying to do what you told her to do. Sleep. And you want to go in and disturb her. She'll think you're nuts.

ME: All right. Good night.

IRVING: Can I count on it?

ME: Yes. Good night. I love you.

IRVING: Me, too. Good night.

(Ten minutes later)

ME: Irving.

IRVING: You know, I should have put you in the kitchen and let her sleep in here with me.

ME: But Irving, she's not out of danger. In fact, the doctor said it was still touch and go.

IRVING: Good night!

(Two minutes later)

IRVING: What do you mean the doctor said it was still touch and go?

ME: The virus is under control. But she's not cured. She could go just like that!

IRVING: Well, for a basket case, she's putting up a pretty brave front.

ME: She's just a baby. She doesn't know how sick
she is. She was also trying very hard to be
charming for you. And now she's too quiet.
She might be suffering, but afraid to call for
help, afraid to get in wrong with you.

IRVING (*getting out of bed*): All right. You stay here.
I'll go and listen at the door.

ME: Irving! You care!

IRVING: Yes. I care about maybe getting a few hours
of sleep.
       (*Two minutes later Irving returns*)

ME: What did you hear?

IRVING (*getting into bed*): Nothing. What did you
expect me to hear? Tap dancing? She's asleep.
I envy her.

ME: But puppies aren't supposed to sleep all night.

IRVING: When I see her in the morning, I'll tell her.

ME: Irving, what shall we do?

IRVING: Well, it may sound ridiculous to you, but *I*
am going to sleep. Right now. Good night!

ME: Well, you don't have to be nasty about it.

IRVING: Would you like me to sleep in the kitchen and
give you and her the bedroom?

ME: Good night!

IRVING: Good night.

(*One hour later—around two* A.M. *I quietly get out
of bed.*)

IRVING (*wide awake, in a deadly voice*): And where
are you going?

ME (*haughtily*): Where do people usually go when
they get out of bed in the middle of the night?

IRVING: I know what people do. But what are your
plans?

ME (*heading for the bathroom*): I am thirsty!
(*then, after returning to bed*): Satisfied? Now,
good night!
              (*Two thirty* A.M.)

ME: Irving, is that you?

IRVING: No, it's Rossano Brazzi.

ME: Where are you going?

IRVING: Maybe it never occurred to you. But I, too, am a people, and *I* am going to the bathroom!

(Three A.M.*)*

ME: Irving, are you asleep?

IRVING: Of course not. I always lie awake all night like this.

ME: Well, she could be dead in there.

IRVING: No such luck!

ME: Good night!

(Five minutes later)

IRVING: Why didn't you ask that doctor whether she should sleep all night?

ME: Well, who thought she would?

(A few minutes tick by)

IRVING *(sitting up)*: Look, I can't stand it. This has got to stop!

ME: I haven't said a word.

IRVING: But you're thinking! I can feel it. And it's keeping me awake.

ME: What would I be thinking?

IRVING: Oh, little things. Like I'm a cold-blooded heel, leaving a helpless little puppy to die alone in the kitchen.

ME *(sitting up)*: Then you think she's dead too!

IRVING: I think I'm married to an idiot. But we might as well go in and see. Then, dead or alive, I'm going to sleep!

(We tiptoe to the kitchen. Irving silently opens the door. Josephine jumps out of her little wicker bed, yawns, wags her tail, then looks at us both expectantly, as if to say, "What's up, Doc?")

IRVING: All right, bring her in.

ME: Bring her in?

IRVING: It's her first night back. Maybe she shouldn't sleep all alone. After all, she did have other dogs at the hospital for company.

(*The three of us finally settle down in the bedroom. Josephine is ecstatic at the change of locale. She covers us both with kisses, and then snuggles in* Irving's *arms and goes to sleep.*)

An hour later, I quietly slid out of bed. This time I really wanted a drink of water. Irving was furious. "For heaven's sake! Haven't you any consideration! You woke her up!"

8

Housebreaking—
and Like That

THIS memorable night was followed by four equally thrilling weeks. I canceled all social engagements, told my agent I was unavailable, and concentrated on playing Florence Nightingale to Josephine's Camille. I also had to be an Olympic champion on the side.

I doubt if Dr. Dafoe spent half the physical energy tending those Dionne quintuplets that I spent tending one three-pound poodle. After all, you plunk a bottle in a baby's mouth and it drinks the milk. Did you ever try plunking some Pepto-Bismol down a poodle's mouth?

The procedure is to place poodle on kitchen sink. With one hand, hold open poodle's mouth. With other hand, pour the lovely pink Pepto-Bismol into mouth. Then drop everything (except poodle, of course) and use both hands to clamp poodle's mouth shut. Then stand helplessly and watch Pepto-Bismol flow gently out of sides of poodle's mouth. (A poodle's mouth has a schizophrenic personality. Example: when poodle gets something in its mouth that poodle wants, poodle's mouth becomes an iron vise; but when poodle gets something put in its mouth that you want, poodle's mouth becomes a sieve.)

But you try again. This time you try for a side-of-the-mouth attack. (Experienced poodle owners swear on this one.) The procedure: clamp poodle's head to

43

one side, using knee action if necessary. Hold entire mouth tightly shut, and sneak in the Pepto-Bismol through a slit near the molars. Then clamp mouth shut and hold position for three minutes. Pepto-Bismol stays down even though poodle's neck will never be the same. Except, five minutes later, as you massage poodle's neck and explain it was for poodle's own good, poodle happily spits up Pepto-Bismol on your blouse. At least that's how it was with Josie and me.

However, if you keep trying, eventually some of the Pepto-Bismol does wind up in the poodle. I wound up with a pink kitchen sink and three pairs of pink polka dotted slacks, but at the end of four weeks, Josephine was functioning normally at both ends.

And I am happy to report that during the four weeks, our little darling ate like a horse. (Of course, we couldn't trust ordinary food on her as yet. She had a prescription-type dog food made up by the doctor, just for her.)

But I never could have survived without the help of *The New York Times* and the *Herald-Tribune*. As far as newspapers go, my own preferences lean toward the *News*, *Mirror*, *Journal*, and *Post*. Let's face it, they have columnists who certainly perk up one's day.

Imagine losing this group and winding up with Arthur Krock and David Lawrence. But I had no choice. The *Times* and *Tribune* completely covered the foyer and kitchen, whereas the smaller papers did not give that wall-to-wall effect. I mean, if you've got to live with newspapers instead of carpets, you don't want a patchwork effect.

Spring came early in April. I stared at the lovely green grass in Central Park. But that's all I did. Stare —from my window. Our purebred gem was not allowed to venture into the damp, unwholesome air for another month. I thought of those healthy figure-firming hikes I had planned for the two of us. Not that I was growing flabby from lack of exercise. There is great indoor sport connected with the raising of a poodle. I lost two inches from my waistline and grew an extra eye in the back of my head.

Of course, if you are planning to redecorate your apartment in the near future, these precautions can be relaxed and you can even feel free to go out for brief periods and leave the poodle and the apartment alone together. But we had just redecorated our apartment. I didn't feel free to brush my teeth unless Josephine was at my side.

Now some of you might say, "Then what is your social life, aside from playing ball and tug of war with the poodle?"

There isn't any. Unless you invite people to come and visit you and the poodle. (Oh, you'll find out who your real friends are soon enough.)

If you do have guests, there are certain rules that must be followed. (That is, if you want to keep the few remaining friends you have.)

1. No matter how fascinating the conversation gets, never allow poodle out of your sight.

2. Be alert to all danger signals.

(A sudden dive under the bed. A sudden peaceful silence. The ominous sound of "crunch crunch.")

The sudden dive under the bed means poodle has taken a delicious bite out of the guest's alligator bag and is determined to finish it. The ominous "crunch crunch" is never a toy or bone poodle is supposed to crunch on. It is always a wire hair roller, razor pack, or bottle of peroxide.

The sudden silence means poodle is planning a devious attack on the out-of-reach mink stole of the guest or her husband's brand-new hat. It's amazing how adept you become in sprinting across the room to rescue a visitor's imported chiffon scarf from those tiny needle-like teeth—the poise you develop as you tell the guest that the hole really *can* be expertly mended. (And keep reminding yourself that it really doesn't matter that the guest is Radie Harris, the Hollywood columnist. You're not in pictures anyway.)

Of course, it is doubly sad that the scarf had to have
been a gift from the late Gertrude Lawrence and that
the shop it came from was bombed during the blitz.

Josie's only "outings" were blanket-wrapped taxi
rides to the doctor's office, where she submitted with
Spartan bravery to the cruel distemper needle. During these visits Josie was treated by various doctors on
the staff. There was a Dr. Grey, Dr. Green, and Dr.
Brown, along with that charmer, Dr. Black. But we
never got lucky and hit Dr. White, whose name was
on the shingle. He was always in surgery.

One day late in April, when the temperature reached
a glorious seventy degrees, I phoned and asked one of
the doctors (I forget which color I got) if I could
take Josie for a short sprint in the park.

He said, "Absolutely not!"

Disconsolately I stared at the park. It was alive with
poodles. I phoned Irving for advice. He suggested I
listen to the doctor. Besides, he wanted to hand over
a healthy dog to Florence Lustig at the end of June.
As you can see, Irving is the type who never breaks
a promise—especially to himself. He also had a cal-
endar on which he had encircled July 1 with red
crayon. On it was written "California" and "D.D.
Day." He was happy to explain that D.D. Day meant
"Dog Departure Day."

I guess that's why I took matters in my own hands
that balmy day in April. We had so little time left.
We must make every minute count. Why should
Florence Lustig's little boy have all the fun and romps
with Josie? I wanted to live too!

I put my thoughts into action. I said, "Josie, we are
going for a walk."

Of course, she didn't know what a "walk" was. She
had never heard the word before, but she knew something was up. She put down the satin throw pillow she
was eating and gave me her undivided attention.

I showed her the leash. (Sure, I had bought a leash. No one had suggested a wheelchair. Who figured I was going to wind up with the Elizabeth Barrett of poodles?) Josie stared at the leash. Something definitely was up. She had never seen that before. She sniffed at it but didn't get the message. However, this dog would do anything for me, so she obligingly tried to eat it. I slipped it around her neck.

She suddenly turned into a whirling dervish. She rolled, leaped, and used all four feet in an effort to free this noose from her neck. It was obvious that, for the first time in our relationship, Josephine and I were having a "difference of opinion."

I picked her up, leash and all, and carried her to the park. I knew she'd get the idea when she saw other dogs sporting similar neckwear. She got the idea after almost choking to death three times. But as soon as she realized that the leash and I were merely an extension of her personality, she relaxed and got into the swing of things.

She smelled the benches, the grass, and even sniffed at the trunks of trees. Then I sat her down and told her the secrets of the grass and trees. They were not merely ornamental. I had plunked down two dollars for her license. That made her a taxpayer. She owned this park. Therefore, the grass and trees were there for her convenience. To be used any time she saw fit. In place of *The New York Times*.

But she didn't seem to get the idea. However, I knew all she needed was a good illustration. I rushed her over to a boxer who was getting set to perform against a litter basket. This was a big mistake. I had expected a performance—not a tidal wave! We both ran for the hills!

Next, I let her view a Scotty as he gently lifted his leg against a tree. She wasn't frightened—just thought it was a disgusting display of bad taste. She watched a wire-haired perform the same ritual, followed by two cocker spaniels and a Maltese terrier. She yawned. After the boxer, all this was chicken feed!

I kept her out for twenty minutes. She enjoyed herself. But that's all she did. Enjoy herself. The moment she reached the privacy of our apartment, she made a dive for the kitchen and *The New York Times*.

However, I wasn't the least disheartened. Josie was very bright. I was positive that after one more outing the *Times* and *Tribune* would lose her patronage. She would have gotten the hang of the park first time out, if only that stupid boxer hadn't come on so strong!

9

The Gourmet

When Irving came home that night, I gave him a complete rundown on "Our Day in the Park." Josie wagged her tail as if to confirm every word I said. The two of us looked so happy that Irving conceded that perhaps a mother's instinct is better than a doctor's. At least this time I had guessed right. Except the next morning Josephine had dysentery.

Naturally, we rushed to the doctor. He gave me a lecture and Josie another shot in the *derrière*. Then he sent us both back to the apartment and the Pepto-Bismol. With Josephine, that Pepto-Bismol is fantastic. Within twenty-four hours she had licked the dysentery. And when I weighed her the following week, she had gained a whole pound.

I began to gaze at the park again. Even the doctor grew optimistic. If nothing unforeseen happened within the next forty-eight hours, we could have another crack at the great outdoors, with official permission. I was delighted. I figured we had it made. The way things were going, how could we miss? She figured a way. She stopped eating.

Just like that. It was a day, just like all the others. I placed the lovely dish of prescription dog food before her and said, "Darling, here's breakfast." Darling walked over, sniffed it, and walked away with a look of disgust.

The same thing happened at lunch, teatime, and dinner. I didn't call the doctor. I took matters into my own hands. I hated doing it to her, but I tried "force feeding." She hated doing it to me, but she tried to choke to death. I called the doctor. He suggested she might need a change at that. Perhaps she was strong enough to go off the special dog food. I could try table scraps. Table scraps?

I explained that I was not in the habit of knocking off a roast beef or turkey on my electric plate. Not only did I have a hotel kitchen, but this kitchen also doubled as her bedroom and bath. The doctor implied that this was my problem. He was a vet, not a chef. And room service was out of the question. Not that I was being chintzy. But room service four times a day? I put the problem to Irving.

At first Irving wasn't interested. He said, "What am I supposed to do? Put on a chef's cap and start tossing flapjacks around in the kitchen?"

But Irving wouldn't just stand around and let someone starve to death. And if Irving wants to, he can be most inventive. He visited the restaurant in our building and called a small but businesslike conference with three of the busboys. A few words were exchanged, some currency passed hands, and within an hour a tremendous bag containing roast beef and filet mignon was delivered to our apartment. Josephine thought it was very tasty. She not only polished off her plate, but begged for more.

Josie thrived on her new diet, and on the first of May, I got the nod from Dr. White's entire staff. With Josie and Central Park, it was "Go" all the way. And oh, how she loved the park. She also loved Fifth Avenue. But she remained true to the *Times* and *Tribune*. This girl was paper-trained, and paper-trained she intended to remain.

A few nights later Madge Evans and her husband, Sidney Kingsley, the playwright, dropped by for a visit. Madge and Sidney adore dogs. They are never caught without two or three. They went into raptures about Josephine. Irving said she was up for grabs the first of July.

Madge stabbed Irving with an icy look. Then she pointed out Josie's assets. Her eyes were oblique and did not bulge. Her coat was going to be magnificent. Her tail was the right length. And her ears were going to be fantastically long. In fact, it was impossible to find fault with her. She was going to be a real prize. Suddenly the prize began to cough.

Madge said, "She coughed."

Sidney said, "Dogs aren't supposed to cough."

I said this dog could do anything. Sidney said he meant that dogs shouldn't cough. If they did, it meant something.

"Like what?"

"Like distemper!"

(And Sidney wrote *Men in White!*)

I wouldn't say this put a damper on the party, but all conversation did stop for a good five minutes. Nothing was heard but an occasional croupy rasp from Josephine, who despite her newest achievement, was in the best of spirits. Between coughs, she kept bringing the ball over for us to toss to her.

No one spoke. We all kind of looked to Sidney to come up with something. Finally, he said, "Do you have a doctor?"

Did I have a doctor? However, the answering service informed me that all the doctors would be in at nine in the morning. No one was at the hospital but sick dogs and the answering service.

Madge and Sidney left after assuring me distemper wasn't always fatal. They knew several dogs who had come through it. Of course, they lost all their teeth and had a slight twitch, but other than that, they were as good as new.

The moment they were gone. Irving took over. He used the positive approach. He knew she was going to

be fine. Why, in the morning the cough would be all
gone. And, having issued this proclamation, he settled
down and lost himself in a thrilling western on the
Late Show.

During the Late Late Show, Josephine's cough developed more tone and resonance. Even Irving began
to show some concern. He switched off the Late Late
Show—a divine musical with Toby Wing.

He stared at her. "Did Madge say she'll lose *all* her
teeth?"

I nodded mournfully.

He sighed. "Oh well, maybe Florence Lustig will
think poodles just come without teeth."

I didn't say a word. I just wondered if I could *really*
convince a jury that it had been a crime of passion.

Then I ran from the room, grabbed Josie, and made
up the bed in the den. (To every married man, this
act has but one meaning: "Tomorrow I'll call my
lawyer, you call yours.") Since it was Josephine Irving wanted to disinherit and not me, he tried to make
amends.

IRVING: Now, don't be silly. You know I love you.

    ME: I haven't distemper. *I* don't need your con-
        cern. She's the one you're heartless about.

JOSEPHINE (*with perfect timing: two rasping coughs.*)

    ME (*rushing to kitchen with Josie*): Here, darling,
        let Mommy give you some honey. It will
        make your throat feel better. (*I pour honey
        down her throat. She likes it.*)

IRVING (*watching this operation*): I had a cough once.
        And you just told me to give up cigarettes.

    ME: You didn't have distemper.

IRVING: How do you know? Come to think of it, I
        did lose a molar that spring. And you know
        my nose twitches once in a while.

    ME: Your nose twitched the day we met.

IRVING: Now come on, put her to sleep in the kitchen,
        we all need a rest.

ME: I can't leave her alone in the kitchen when I
      know she has distemper.

IRVING: You don't know anything of the sort.

ME: Sidney says so.

IRVING: Just because Sidney wrote *Men in White*
      doesn't mean he's a diagnostic veterinarian.

ME: He did research. He knows.

IRVING: He also wrote *Detective Story*, but I don't
      think J. Edgar Hoover calls him every morn-
      ing for advice.

(*With that, he picks up Josephine and places her in
her little wicker basket. Josie licks his hand and blissfully goes to sleep.*)

Bright and early the following morning, Josie and
I were at Dr. White's hospital. This time we drew a
Dr. Silver. Dr. White was in surgery. Dr. Silver studied
her ten-page case history. He sent for Dr. Black.

After a thorough checkup, Dr. Black assured me it
was not distemper. It was all part of her "condition."
Although the virus was under control, it was by no
means cured. Now it had settled in her upper respira-
tory system. The cough would last until she was six
months old. Then either she or the cough would dis-
appear. As the familiar wild look came into my eyes,
he stopped me with a warning gesture.

"Mrs. Mansfield, I never guaranteed that this girl
would live to a ripe old age. It's a miracle that she
pulled through the initial onslaught. If she continues
to gain weight and strength, and gets past the sixth
month, she'll make it. Meanwhile, she's still very un-
derweight. Now go home and get some meat on this
pup."

As Josie and I stalked out of the room, he added,
"And it wouldn't hurt you to get some flesh on your
own bones."

"I'm on television," I retorted. "I have to stay thin."

"Well, if you want to starve yourself, that's your

business. But don't plan on making her another Lassie. Get some fat on that dog!"

I merely tossed him a glare. As Irving says, "Everyone's in show business!"

10

On Giving Up
The New York Times

Aɴᴅ so we settled down and learned to live with the cough. And from the way things were going, it looked as if we were going to have to learn to live with *The New York Times*. I don't know whether Josephine was stubborn or shy, but she continued to regard Central Park as a recreation hall rather than a public lavatory.

But all in all, May was an exciting month. Josephine had her first poodle haircut and the restaurant in our building closed for renovation. I don't know who took it harder, the busboys or me. Irving solved that problem with a quick visit to Danny's Hideaway. Danny was delighted to take over as Josephine's new chef.

But there was nothing Irving could do about the haircut which he regarded as a catastrophe. He claimed I had turned an innocent-looking puppy into an outlandish freak. Then he topped it off with, "No wonder she clings to *The New York Times*. With that haircut, she's ashamed to be seen outdoors."

I said she had been outdoors for a month without a haircut and nothing happened.

He said, "That's because you're making such a project out of it. It's all your fault she doesn't get the message about Central Park. You've developed such an anxiety complex over it, you've transferred it to her."

"I suppose you could do better!"

"Any time," he snapped.

That did it. I shrieked, "If you're so brilliant and adjusted, I'd like to see you show her why God made a tree!"

And, by God, it worked. Impelled by blind, stupid male ego, he shouted, "Watch me!" He grabbed Josie and her pink rhinestone leash and dashed out of the apartment. It all happened so fast that I think it was more reflex action rather than an actual decision on his part.

All of my anger disappeared as I sat with a smug smile, envisioning his horror when reality set in and he found himself out in broad daylight, sporting a naked poodle with red hair ribbons on its ears. When five minutes had passed and he hadn't returned, I felt a glow of happiness. Maybe he had succeeded, and he was proud of her. When fifteen minutes had passed and there was still no sign of him, I was positively ecstatic. When an hour had passed, I was ready to call the police.

Before taking this drastic step, I called my friends. They tried to reassure me. Irving was very good about watching traffic lights. Every day he made it to his office and back without getting hit by a bus or falling through a manhole. This made good sense. I waited another hour.

I was taking my third Miltown when I heard the key in the lock. In actual count, they had been gone three hours and twelve minutes. Josephine rushed to *The New York Times* ready to explode. Irving stood gazing at her with a stupid grin. I asked where they had been. Did he have any success with the trees? (It seemed obvious that he hadn't, as I mopped up the flooded kitchen floor.) Didn't he realize how worried I had been? Where had they gone? But all he did was stand there with that stupid smile.

Finally, he spoke. "Wow! Is she a conversation piece!"

I didn't stop to ask what he meant because the "conversation piece" had suddenly collapsed on the floor and was snoring! And six-month-old puppies don't snore. Irving said maybe it was because she had walked about sixty blocks. As I massaged her paws with oil, I asked if he was trying to kill her.

He retained that idiotic grin as he gave me the explanation. It seems that on every block at least three or four beautiful girls stopped and said, "Oh, what an adorable dog." Naturally, he had to be polite and stop so they could pet her. Then, of course, they asked her name. And when he said, "Josie Mansfield," several of the girls said, "Oh, are you Irving Mansfield, the TV producer?" (Well, it seems most of the girls had those big bags and picture folios—they were models and just dying to go on TV. So they told him their names, and, naturally, all this took time.) I said I couldn't recall seeing Central Park crawling with high-fashion models.

It seems they had bypassed Central Park. It was wet in the park and Irving had on his new Italian moccasins. Besides, as he put it, Park Avenue is just loaded with trees.

And that's how it went. The more he walked, the more people he talked with. He even talked with a few people he knew. Like Rudolph Bing.

"But you don't know Rudolph Bing." I was positive of that.

"I do now. His dog got on very intimate sniffing terms with Josie."

Then he stretched on the couch to rest. Maybe he expected me to rub *his* feet with olive oil. But I just sat there and fumed. Worrying me to death while he was out enjoying himself with my dog!

Suddenly he said, "Oh, next time you have Josie clipped, tell them to try yellow hair ribbons. Jayne Mansfield said yellow would look wonderful on her." Jayne Mansfield!

"She stopped to admire Josie." I didn't say a word. I just stared.

He got defensive. "What should I have done? Throw rocks at her? Besides, Jayne is a poodle owner. Her Bobo is pink."

"What?"

"Her poodle. Bobo. She uses vegetable dye on him." (How could I have lived without this piece of information?)

"There's nothing wrong with making small talk with poodle owners, or poodle admirers," he explained. "It's socially acceptable. Like talking to strangers on board ship."

And it went on and on. He was just bursting with little goodies. Just as I thought we had about covered it, he said, "Next time you have her clipped, tell the guy to try silver nail polish. Zsa Zsa says—"

"Zsa Zsa who?"

He smiled with indulgent good humor. "Zsa Zsa has a Maltese terrier and she said . . ."

That night I took a seconal. I dozed off with his voice still floating to me in the dark. The last thing I recall was how Josie adored other dogs. Especially that cute Chihuahua that belonged to Abbe Lane!

11

D.D. Day

THE NEXT DAY *I* tried Park Avenue. After all, I wanted to live, too. And I had read that both Cary Grant and Tony Curtis were in town. Well, Irving hadn't exaggerated. Josie sure was a smash. Like he said, we were stopped by every beautiful model. They all wanted to cuddle Josie. Since this wasn't exactly what I had in mind, I decided to try another avenue. I figured Madison Avenue might be different. It was. I spent ten minutes having a thrilling tête-à-tête with Arthur Murray. And on the next block I ran into Charles Coburn. You can see how my luck was running.

Thereafter I confined our walks to Central Park. At least there we'd meet dogs, and Josie might learn about the trees. But Josephine seemed to have a closed mind on this subject. I pointed out all the other dogs who dutifully lifted well-trained legs against the waiting trees. Josephine stared obediently, and sometimes even displayed a small amount of interest, but she never regarded it as anything but a spectator sport.

I coaxed. I pleaded. I finally resorted to physical instruction. I lifted her leg against a tree and held it there for ten minutes. I had no results other than to attract a curious group of onlookers. However, I stuck to it relentlessly. My motto: "Let them stop and stare, it won't bother me."

It got so I became a familiar sight in the park, holding Josie's leg against a tree. After a few days, I rarely attracted more than a passing stare.

One day, while I was in the midst of this new hobby, a fat woman with two pregnant Airedales passed. She paused to stare at me with interest.

After about ten minutes, she said, "What is she supposed to be doing?" (Oh, you meet all kinds! What did she think Josephine was supposed to be doing? Ballet exercises?) But I couldn't be rude to a fat lady with two pregnant dogs, so I gave her a brief explanation.

The fat lady said, "But she's a girl."

I agreed and returned my attention to Josie and the tree. Josie, who has the disposition of an angel, obediently held her leg up, but of course, nothing happened. (I tell you, that dog would do anything for me, except give up *The New York Times*.)

The fat lady stood there and studied the situation with great interest. Finally she said, "Girls don't lift their legs against trees."

I put down Josie's leg. What did girl dogs do?

She said, "They squat."

Then, as if on command, her fat Airedales squatted and showed me how it was done. Even Josephine watched with interest, although she seemed slightly embarrassed at their lack of restraint. Then the fat lady and her Airedales waddled off with the air of personal satisfaction of a job well done.

The moment they were out of sight, I tried to push Josie into a squatting position. She went rigid and stared at me like I had suddenly lost my senses. The more I tried, the more rigid she became.

That night I told Irving about my conversation with the fat lady. He said it made sense and agreed to give it a whirl. The following morning we took her to the park together. After three or four unsuccessful attempts on my part, Irving snatched her from me. What was I trying to do to this poor dog? First I had almost gotten her leg out of joint. Now she was a cinch for curvature of the spine.

He decided to take over. He sent me home, promising he wouldn't return until he could report "mission accomplished." But he'd let her do it her way. She could either lift her leg, sit, squat, or stand on her ear. But it would come about on her own, without any physical instruction from him or advice from demented spectators. When he took her for a walk, he was discriminating. When they stopped to chat, that's all they did, chat. And with attractive people. They didn't go around taking advice or getting involved with total strangers. An hour later he and Josie returned. They both looked radiant.

I rushed to him. "She lifted her leg!"

He shook his head.

"She squatted?"

He gave me a bored look. "Can't you get your thoughts out of the bathroom?"

"Then what did she do?"

He smiled. "She got engaged."

"To whom?"

"Bobo Eichenbaum."

"Who is he?"

"A poodle."

"A poodle!" I was stunned.

He shrugged. "Well, you might prefer Gregory Peck. But she is perfectly willing to settle for a poodle."

I tried to explain. Our little angel still didn't even know about the birds and the trees—and here he was, rushing her into marriage.

He told me to relax. They weren't planning to elope over the weekend. They'd have the usual courtship, get to know one another real well, then, she'd pick the date. It was really fate because Bobo lived in our hotel. On the fourth floor.

The following day I did a little private checking on

my future son-in-law's background. The bellboys and chambermaids gave me a complete rundown. Bobo was a very nice, refined black poodle. Bobo's family owned loan companies, golf ranges, and several hotels in Florida. In fact, Bobo sounded like just the kind of man all my unmarried girl friends were searching for —too bad he was a poodle.

I decided to phone Mrs. Eichenbaum to explain why Josephine had to reject the "catch" of the season. Using my most folksy voice, I explained to Mrs. Eichenbaum that I had never met Bobo, so there was nothing personal in what I was about to say. But the engagement was off! Josephine was not going to get married. In fact, Josephine was *never* going to get married. First, there was her delicate physical condition. By the time I got through with Josephine's medical past, Liz Taylor's famous bout with pneumonia sounded like a mere head cold.

During this monologue, I had tried three different pronunciations of Eichenbaum. I figure at least two of them had to be wrong, but Mrs. Eichenbaum never interrupted me. In fact, if it hadn't been for her steady breathing, I might have doubted that she was still on the line. When I finished, Mrs. Eichenbaum showed the first sign of life. She cleared her throat.

Then she spoke. "First things first. The name is Eichenbaum. Since it's going to be your daughter's name some day, you might as well learn how to pronounce it. Just remember it this way. There's the A bomb, the H bomb and we're the Eichen baums."

I told her that as long as I lived I would never forget her name, but, I reiterated, Josie was not going to get married.

After a slight pause Mrs. Eichenbaum inquired, "Tell me, don't you like marriage?"

I said I adored marriage. Especially with Irving. "Then why can't my Bobo marry Josephine?"

I decided Mrs. Eichenbaum deserved a full explanation. First I confided my immediate problem. Florence Lustig and her little boy.

Mrs. Eichenbaum faded me with a sympathetic "Tch Tch."

I went on to explain that if a miracle did happen and Irving let me keep Josie, I certainly couldn't push my luck and expect him to accept her children.

"But he was all for the marriage," Mrs. Eichenbaum insisted.

"Sure. He figured she'd go to live with you."

Mrs. Eichenbaum thought this over. "I wouldn't mind," she conceded.

"But I would," I shouted. "I want Josephine with me. And if she had children, I couldn't bear to give any of them away, because they would be her children."

I finally got through to Mrs. Eichenbaum. "Oh, I see. So if you're not going to keep the poodles, you see no reason to make her go through childbirth."

I said that was it exactly.

"But you could sell the poodles." Mrs. Eichenbaum was the practical type.

"Would you sell your daughter's poodles?" I demanded.

"No. I'd give them to my nephews." Then she went on to qualify this statement. "I want Bobo to get married. My nephews all want poodles. As the mother of the groom, I get either a stud fee or the pick of the litter."

"And as the mother of the bride, what would I get?"

"A pregnant poodle."

"Who made these rules?" I was outraged.

Mrs. Eichenbaum said the A.K.C. made these rules. Of course she didn't want any stud fee. She just wanted the pick of the litter. After all, she had to get at least one of her nephews started.

Now I was curious. "What would happen if Josephine had only one poodle?"

"It would go to my nephew."

I was disgusted. It really is a man's world. Our little darling was supposed to do all the work while Bobo stood around handing out cigars and poodles!

I said, "Well, it was nice talking to you," and started to take leave of Mrs. Eichenbaum.

Mrs. Eichenbaum said, "What's your rush? We haven't solved your biggest problem yet. Between us, we should be able to figure out some scheme to fix it so you can keep Josephine."

That made me feel wonderful. I may have lost a son-in-law, but I had gained a friend. I said I was open for suggestions. Mrs. Eichenbaum had none at the moment, although she hinted that she'd give up Mr. Eichenbaum before she'd part with Bobo. However, she pointed out that I did have a whole month to go. And many things could happen in a month. And on that happy note, we parted.

But June passed very quickly. Before I knew it, D.D. Day was just forty-eight hours away. I grew very depressed. Even Josie knew something was up. She did everything to please me. She even stopped coughing. In fact she had stopped coughing for three days. I pointed out this fact to Irving. She had passed the hump. She was going to live a good long life—but with whom?

I didn't know where I stood. If I wanted to look at it hopefully, we had only forty-eight hours to go, and he hadn't mentioned Florence Lustig and her little boy for a whole week. If I wanted to look at it realistically—he had already purchased our plane tickets for California and hadn't even tried to apply for permission to take Josephine on the plane. (And I had checked, you needed permission.)

Well, I wasn't going to bring up the subject. Let him suffer through it. He knew I always kept a promise, and I had promised that when D.D. Day arrived, I would hand Josie over without any recriminations or traumas.

Oh, I would be a brick about it. And I wouldn't really hold it against him. Of course I wouldn't talk to him for a month or two, but I would keep my promise: no hysterics on D.D. Day. However, I was determined to let him bring it up. He did. That night in Sardi's.

He had ordered a chocolate parfait (his favorite dessert).

I had ordered nothing. I wasn't hungry.

He said, "Well, you just can't sit there."

I said, "Watch me."

His parfait arrived. He said, "Looks great, doesn't it? Sure you won't change your mind?"

I shook my head. Five minutes passed in dreadful silence.

Suddenly he said, "Florence Lustig has taken a lovely place at Long Beach for the summer."

I said that was very nice.

He said, "Have one spoon of my parfait."

I shook my head.

He said, "Sardi's makes marvelous parfaits."

I looked at it. "Then why haven't you touched it?"

He stared. "I'm not hungry." He beckoned the waiter to take away the melting parfait. Then we were both silent.

Suddenly he said, "Look, even if we wanted to take her with us, the Beverly Hills Hotel doesn't allow dogs."

I couldn't believe my ears. "Irving! You don't want to give her away!"

He nodded. "Of course I don't. But what do we do with her over the summer? I can't tell Florence Lustig she's just a house guest. Besides, it wouldn't be fair to her little boy. He'd get so attached to her, he'd never give her up."

"Well, we could put her in a kennel," I explained. "There are several good ones in Westchester. Or, we could even take her to California and put her in a kennel there—and then there is Mr. Ingram."

He stared at me. "For a girl who expected to part with her dog, you sure are a bundle of information. Or did this all just come to you in a flash?"

I smiled and snuggled against him.

Then he said, "Who is Mr. Ingram?"

"Mr. Ingram takes certain dogs into his home. They have to be 'name' dogs, preferably show business dogs. He's had Myrna Loy's dog, Polly Bergen's dog, Merv Griffin's dog. He gives them the run of his house, just as if they were his dogs. If they want to sleep with him, they can. But he's very expensive."

"Expensive like what?" Irving asked.

"Expensive like five dollars a day."

Irving gave me a cold stare. "If *we* can afford the Beverly Hills Hotel, *she* can afford Mr. Ingram!"

Tears came to my eyes. I just said, "Oh Irving, I love you so!"

He went on. "Call this Mr. Ingram tomorrow. I want to see him. If my dog is going to spend the summer at his home, I want to see his references."

We both smiled blissfully and he ordered another parfait, with two spoons.

12

Family Reunion

We MISSED Josie that summer, but Mr. Ingram kept us posted on her activities. She was healthy and happy, he assured us. At the end of the summer I dropped him a note to inform him of the date of our return. However, since we were due to land at midnight, I said he could wait until the following morning to deliver Josephine.

I enjoyed the flight home. It was turbulent, but it didn't bother me. Fear of flying is all in the mind. It's easy to conquer. Just tell yourself that the pilot does know what he is doing, the plane has been tested and is foolproof. Hold these thoughts in mind, take two sleeping pills and a bottle of beer, and you'll find flying can be fun!

When we arrived at Idlewild, I perched on the most comfortable bench and prepared to let Irving go through the usual hassle to get our baggage. To my amazement, he headed in the opposite direction and entered a phone booth. I strolled over. Naturally I was interested.

He was talking to Mr. Ingram! Announcing his intentions to stop by and pick up our little darling. Obviously, Mr. Ingram had other intentions at that hour of the night, because Irving's voice took on a slight edge.

"What do you mean, everyone is sleeping? It's only ten after twelve. Josie never goes to sleep before two or three in the morning."

There was a slight pause. Mr. Ingram evidently was trying to explain his unconventional hours.

Irving remained adamant. "Mr. Ingram, I don't care what Mrs. Mansfield wrote. We are picking her up tonight!"

He stalked out of the booth, the victorious warrior, tossing me a glance that plainly said, "Some mother you are!"

For once, I took one of his "looks" lying down. Secretly, I was impressed with this new parental attitude. It must have impressed Mr. Ingram also. When we pulled up in front of his residence, he was standing on the street with a coat over his pajamas and Josie in his arms. Josie went into hysterical delight at the sight of us. She dismissed Mr. Ingram with a fickle flip of her tail and began to passionately bestow hundreds of rough little kisses on both our faces.

Mr. Ingram stared at her adoringly. "She's really quite a dog. Of all the dogs who have stayed with us, not one of them has her charm or personality." (She had hooked Mr. Ingram too!) Yet she never even tossed him a wave of her paw as our taxi drove away! She was too busy showering us with assembly-line kisses, which did not let up until the taxi neared our hotel. Then she stopped kissing to emit a few murmurs of pleasure.

Irving was amazed. "She recognizes the neighborhood!"

And when we pulled up to the hotel, she leaped out of the cab, dragged us to the curb, and squatted! We almost fainted with pride!

Irving made the doorman and the bellboy stop unloading the baggage and watch. He exclaimed on the marvel of it to the cab driver. Only eight months old and so brilliant!

We ran into Bobo Eichenbaum and his family in the lobby. Irving told them about the curb bit. Mr. Eichenbaum agreed that it was simply marvelous. He was a little disturbed about Bobo. It seems Bobo squatted too. Only boys are not supposed to squat. Mrs. Eichenbaum rushed to Bobo's defense. She said she was sure it was just because Bobo was so young and innocent. She was positive there was no deeper reason.

Irving, who is sometimes brutally frank, said, "Personally, I've always thought he was a fag."

Mrs. Eichenbaum was shocked, but Mr. Eichenbaum took a realistic approach. He said, "I've told Mrs. Eichenbaum he shouldn't wear those yellow hair ribbons."

"He looks gorgeous in them," Mrs. Eichenbaum insisted. "Besides, even if he squats, his instincts are normal. Look at him with Josephine."

We looked at him. He was sitting up on his hind legs, pleading for Josie's attention. Then fate intervened and a series of events followed that caused no one to challenge Bobo's masculinity. Another poodle arrived on the scene. He was a darling black and white pari named Brandy. He hailed from Texas and had just checked into the hotel. He took one look at Josie and swooned.

Josie looked at him but got no message. Bobo sat there begging. Brandy became a bit more aggressive. He took a small sniff at Josie. Bobo stopped begging and cocked his head. Brandy sniffed again. Bobo couldn't believe his eyes. Brandy became openly amorous. Bobo tried to kill Brandy!

It all happened so fast. The sudden lunge Bobo made at Brandy's throat, the whirling mass of the two dogs—both shrieking and snarling. The lobby was in an uproar. Two bellboys, Mr. Eichenbaum, Irving, and Brandy's father dived in to separate them, while Mrs. Eichenbaum stood and hollered at the top of her lungs. I held Josephine and also shouted for help. I was positive neither dog would survive. Josephine watched the proceedings with a detached sort of interest.

The two dogs were finally separated. Bobo's lip was

bleeding and Brandy had lost a large patch of fur near
his throat. Other than that, no real damage was done.
Brandy was hustled out for air, and Mrs. Eichenbaum
sat puffing on the couch while Mr. Eichenbaum
soothed the courageous Bobo.

Josephine snuggled on the sofa and fell sound asleep.
Mrs. Eichenbaum stared at her with contempt. "Look
what they both almost killed themselves over. And
she couldn't care less."

I grabbed Josie and made a hasty retreat toward the
elevator. Josie never so much as favored poor Bobo
with a good-night nod, which probably inspired Mrs.
Eichenbaum to come up with her final bon mot.

"Imagine being a siren with that figure!"

I stopped dead at the elevator. "What's wrong with
her figure?"

"She hasn't any figure! Look at that belly, it's
enormous!"

Irving and I didn't say a word all the way up in
the elevator. But the moment we were alone in the
apartment, we took inventory of our pride and joy.
Mrs. Eichenbaum did have a point. Josie no longer
had that wonderful concave look.

Irving sprang to her defense. "She's not fat. She just
needs a haircut. After all, she does have a magnificent
coat."

On her belly? Well, he did have to admit that from
her rib cage on she didn't go up, like Bobo or Brandy.
As he saw it, from her rib cage on, she was straight.
As I saw it, from her rib cage on, she hung.

He argued that maybe girl poodles were supposed to
look that way. Didn't they have ten or eleven bosoms?
Besides, there was nothing attractive about a skinny
girl. All great beauties were amply endowed. Look
at Sophia Loren and Anita Ekberg!

I said that Grace Kelly was thin and had managed
to get by. Grace Kelly was a different type, he insisted. Josie was a brunette—the voluptuous, full-
blown type like Liz Taylor.

Well, only a fool would fight a statement like that. Besides, I was tired. And I am also a brunette. And if he thought Josie looked like Sophia Loren and Liz Taylor, why should I point out any minor discrepancies? After all, he was paying her bills, not Mrs. Eichenbaum.

13

Calories *Do* Count!

IRVING'S glamorous explanation of Josephine's ample waistline lulled me into a false sense of security. During the fall and winter our full-blown beauty continued to bloom. Soon I began to regard her chubbiness as part of her sparkling personality. It got so I didn't even bat an eye when the bellboys greeted her fondly with "Hello Chubby." And when dog-loving strangers passed us on the street and said, "There's a little fatty," I just took it in my stride.

Of course, none of my good friends ever said she was fat. I don't know whether they were blind or just valued my friendship. I'm sure Bea Cole would never have mentioned it intentionally. It just sort of slipped out. After all, Bea is one of my oldest and dearest friends.

We were sitting around playing ball with Josie one afternoon. I told Bea there was the possibility that Irving and I might have to make a short trip to California and I was weighing the advantages of taking Josie along or leaving her with Mr. Ingram.

Bea said, "Why can't she stay with us? It was different last summer when she was so little and still sickly, but now she's a year old and housebroken, it'd be a cinch."

When I didn't answer, Bea said, "Don't you trust me with Josie?"

"Oh, I trust you. It's Karen that worries me." (Karen was Bea's five-year-old daughter.)

"Karen loves dogs."

"I'm sure she does. But Bea, children regard dogs as playthings. She would be rough without meaning it. You know, accidentally step on Josie or drop her. She doesn't know how fragile poodles are."

It was then that Bea came up with the blockbuster! "Fragile! The way Josie's going, I'd be afraid she'd crush Karen!"

My voice was deadly. "Are you intimating that Josie is fat?"

Bea didn't give an inch. "I'm intimating that Josie's new winter coat will have to be custom-made by Lane Bryant!"

For ten seconds a lifelong friendship wavered precariously. Then logic overcame emotion and I realized Bea meant well. I studied Josephine. "Maybe I should try a new kind of haircut."

Bea remained adamant. "I think you should try a waist nipper and a course at Vic Tanny's."

I decided to try the haircut first. The following day I rushed Josie to Poodle Boutique. I told Mel Davis, who grooms her, to do away with the Dutch Clip she usually wore. The padded shoulders and hips made her look too heavy.

Mel studied her. "I could give her the Sport Clip. Shear her entire body and just leave the legs full, but it wouldn't be as flattering. The broad shoulders and rear minimize the thickness of her waist."

Mel too? I asked him if he really thought she was fat.

Mel was diplomatic. "She's chubby in the midsection. But I think it's part of her personality." (Josie was not only a good customer, but a heavy tipper.) I told him to give her the Sport Clip.

At five o'clock I arrived to pick her up. Mel greeted me with a funny look. In fact, everyone in the shop looked strange. Except Josephine. She looked ridiculous. For a moment, no one spoke. Then Mel came up with the understatement of all time.

"I think the Dutch Cut was more flattering."

I didn't say a word. I was wondering whether Ira Senz could fashion some kind of a poodle toupee—for her belly. Although Josephine is a brunette, her skin is snow white. Without the shoulder fur, the first thing that hit you was her belly. Gleaming and white. Stark and unrelieved. No hanging fur to hide its shining splendor.

Mel spoke again. "Maybe she has a tumor," he offered hopefully.

She had to have something! I rushed right over to Dr. White's. We got Dr. Blue. (Dr. White was in surgery.) Dr. Blue took one look at her and called in Dr. Black and Dr. Green. They all stared. Someone suggested edema. Someone suggested malfunctioning of the kidneys. Everyone suggested an immediate X-ray.

Five minutes later I got the verdict. No tumor. No edema. Just fat! She must go on a diet immediately. No more Yummies, tidbits, or milkbones—only one meal a day!

"One meal a day?"

"One meal a day consisting of eight ounces of ground meat," Dr. Black announced.

I explained that eight ounces of anything was just an hors d'oeuvre to Josie.

When they came up with little statements about fat pressing against her heart, asthmatic attacks, pneumonia, I stopped arguing. I was convinced. Now all I had to do was to convince Irving. And Josie.

I had a rough time with Irving. The haircut alone threw him into a state of shock. And when I got to the eight ounces of chopped meat, he really blew. He accused me of just going around and looking for trouble. He didn't care what Bea Cole thought. She was a lovely girl and a good actress, but this didn't qualify her to become Josie's dietitian. As for the doctors at Dr. White's hospital—naturally they wanted her thin. Then they could give her build-up shots after she became anemic. One meal a day? What happened to breakfast? Did the doctors know we were theatrical people? Did they know Josie kept our hours, that she always rose at noon and couldn't start her day until she had her second saucer of coffee?

I explained that Dr. Blue said thin people lived longer. Irving said that was a fallacy. He pointed out that Sophie Tucker was well into her seventies and worked fifty-two weeks a year, did two shows a night, and between shows, sold her records to promote money for a camp for underprivileged children. Could Dr. Blue do that?

Then I explained about the asthma and the fat pressing against her heart. Even though Josie was built like Sophie—maybe it was different with dogs. This had a sobering effect upon Irving. And when we sat down to have a Scotch, he didn't even put down her usual plate of salted peanuts. No more coffee; no more Yummies; no more peanuts, potato chips, and caviar. No more meals from Danny's Hideaway or cannelloni from Sardi's.

Yes, that was her life. And now all that rich living had to end!

14

The Family Circle

IT LASTED for exactly forty-eight hours. Then, on a Friday night at six P.M. Irving arrived carrying a hot freshly roasted chicken. Chicken is her favorite dish.

She started doing a Charleston around the bag, while Irving made these cooing noises: "Look what the Daddy brought home for you. The Mother wants to starve you. Just because the Mother is on TV and thinks it's stylish to look consumptive, she's not going to starve my dog."

I was outraged. Because Josephine does understand every word you say, and a little speech like this could turn her against me. I tried to explain to both of them that rich living would be her destruction. And to remember what the doctor said about fat and cholesterol.

Josie dismissed my ravings with an icy stare and gave Irving her full attention along with little murmurs of ecstacy which she directed toward the fragrant bag. Irving unwrapped the chicken and tenderly finger-fed it to her (so no bones would get in the way). Of course, he had a logical explanation for this uncalled for gastronomic delight.

"She'll diet tomorrow. But this is Friday night."

"What's so special about Friday night?"

"When I was a boy in Brooklyn, everyone had chicken on Friday night."

"But she's not a boy in Brooklyn. She's an over-weight French poodle on Central Park South."

But I wasn't getting through to him—or to her. Besides, as he put it, maybe it was her nature to be heavy. He felt she definitely took after his side of the family. She was built exactly like his mother. Small boned, but large in the tummy.

Naturally, I relayed this information to his mother, a darling woman, who accepted this compliment with a slightly glazed look. I cannot say enough about my mother-in-law. Suffice to say, she was never a mother-in-law, but one of the most gentle and self-sacrificing women I have ever known and one of the best friends I ever had. But to her, animals were animals. Not relatives. Animals belonged in the jungle or a zoo. Horses belonged on television, or under policemen. Cats were created to eat mice. And dogs—well, maybe dogs ate cats. But dogs who ate chicken and went to beauty parlors, this was a new way of life.

On the day of our marriage, she hugged me and said she had gained a daughter rather than lost a son. And she had always wanted a daughter. Yet she failed to show any enthusiasm about her newest acquisition —a four-legged, pot-bellied granddaughter.

Instead, she seemed slightly concerned about the state of Irving's mental health. She and her husband had suffered through the depression of the thirties and had deprived themselves of many things to put Irving through high school and college. And he had not let them down. She was proud of his success, but she never went around boasting about it. She felt his record could speak for itself. To her, it was a conceded fact that he was more handsome than Ronald Colman. (Don't start in about Cary Grant, Robert Taylor, and the others. She liked Ronald Colman.)

And when Irving corrected her totaling of monthly bills and explained the mysteries of balancing a checkbook, she said Einstein was lucky that Irving had chosen show business as a career instead of metaphysics. And then, to suddenly see her remarkable son transformed into the father of a poodle, and talking baby talk to this poodle, must have caused her many moments of secret anguish.

But as I have stated, she was a remarkable woman. She didn't blame this idiotic transformation on me. She just made some innocuous remarks like: "Every man is master of his own destiny" and "If a grown man with a college education is happy playing nurse-maid to a poodle, why should I butt in." She also said it was very nice that we thought we were Mommy and Daddy to the poodle. But did the poodle think we were Mommy and Daddy or just two excellent servants who were created for no other purpose than to feed her and attend to her every desire. But if it made us happy, that's all that mattered. But she did drop a little hint about Uncle Louis on Irving's father's side who wasn't too bright and had gotten a little feeble-minded as he grew older. Not that anything like this was inherited, but it never hurt to have a checkup.

She also made it perfectly clear that she had nothing personal against Josephine. She even sided with Irving about Josie's build. A little extra flesh never hurt anyone. And of course, chicken on Friday nights was an accepted fact.

She never offered any advice or asked personal questions. The only time this marvelous woman showed even the slightest sign of displeasure occurred on one of her weekly visits when I attempted to cement a closer grandmother-granddaughter relationship. I held Josie up to her face as she entered the door and cooed, " Josie, Grandma's here. Kiss Grandma."

Naturally, Josie obliged. And wanting to make a good impression, she really put her heart into it. She began to studiously wash Grandma's face—veil and all.

Grandma backed away and said gently, "Couldn't she call me Annie?" I got the message and stopped with the Grandma.

15

The Trouble with Being
a Magnificent Brunette

It was in the spring that we proudly realized she had developed into a real tearing beauty. Everyone said that about Josie. In fact her beauty was so overpowering, you scarcely noticed the slight bulge in her waistline. Her ears were shoulder length. Her teeth were like ivory. And her eyes were soft and more beautiful than sable. And her hair (technically called coat) was blue-black, abundant, and naturally curly. If I weren't so mad about her, I might have resented her. Especially when Irving stared at her, then at me, and said, "You know, before Josie, I always thought *your* hair was black." Then he looked at her wistfully. "Wouldn't it be nice if we had some pictures?"

I nodded. After that we both plunged into a deep silence.

Finally I spoke. "I could call Bruno of Hollywood. I'm sure he'd do it."

He thought about it. "Bruno is great for you. But maybe there's a photographer who specializes in dogs."

I said, "I'll look into it."

He said, "Do that."

Then we dropped the subject immediately. We always steer clear of dangerous subjects. Subjects that deal with one or the other's shortcomings. With Irving, photography is a shortcoming. With me, it's total disaster!

Irving and I have real "togetherness." We have "togetherness" with golf, friends, and careers. Unfortunately, we even have "togetherness" in being inflicted with brains that automatically refuse to function when they come in contact with certain technical and electronic gadgets.

You can leave Irving on his own to produce the most complicated television show, and he's a winner. But leave him on his own to refill a cigarette lighter and he's a calculated risk!

I still remember that beautiful leather cigarette lighter George S. Kaufman gave us one Christmas. It worked like a torch for about three weeks. Then, as cigarette lighters will, it ran dry. Irving said, "I'll refill it." If any other husband made a similar statement, the wife would nod and turn her attention to other matters.

But Irving said it! And it was a beautiful lighter. I rushed and grabbed the lighter. "Please, Irving, don't touch it. I'll call the hotel electrician."

He brushed me aside and took the lighter. "It's going to be all right this time. I stopped at Dunhill's and they gave me detailed instructions. Once you learn all the facts, it's really quite simple."

I must say he spoke with a new kind of authority, and even his attack on the project was professional and reassuring. First he removed his jacket. Then he rolled up his sleeves. He took a Turkish towel and spread it across the table. He motioned me to stay out of his light. With the precision of a surgeon lining up his instruments, he placed a dime, a bottle of lighter fluid, and an eyebrow tweezer on the towel, neatly in a row. (In spite of myself, I was getting impressed.)

He fit the dime into the screw at the bottom. And before I could say, "Irving, maybe you shouldn't," the thing was apart.

He hadn't just opened it, he had disemboweled it! Wires, doodads, and all kinds of things dropped to the table. But it didn't seem to bother him. With calm assurance, he took the tweezer and pulled up the wick. Then, like a surgeon addressing his gallery, he said, "That's to give it a higher flame."

He put down the tweezer and calmly opened the can of lighter fluid. He turned the lighter over to add the fluid. Suddenly, he stopped dead.

"There's cotton in here." I looked. There certainly was.

"But no one told me about the cotton."

"Ignore it," I pleaded. "You're doing beautifully." I tried not to look at all the wires and doodads that were still lying on the table.

He inserted the new flints, but I noticed his hands trembled a bit. That cotton had really rocked him. As he began to put the lighter into the case and replace the coils, I could see the confidence literally ebb out of him. But he saw it through. And he really did an excellent job. He stuffed everything back into the lighter except for one or two little coils. He even got the screw in place with the dime. It looked marvelous. Except that it wouldn't light.

He stared at it for a moment, then walked to the window, opened it, took a deep breath, and with all his strength, hurled the lighter out into space.

What did I do? What any good wife would do. I tossed away the extra coils and closed the window. This is the story of the cigarette lighter and us. Can you imagine us with a camera?

Oh, I could go on and on explaining how we almost got electrocuted with the automatic coffee pot. How we put the entire hotel in darkness when we just turned on our air conditioner for the first time. But why bore you with our little scientific mishaps. Irving not only looks upon John Glenn as a god, manipulating all those levers, but he also has a sound respect for that monkey who took the test flight. And I agree. Because no matter how many bananas you fed Irving, he'd never push the right levers!

So when it came to having Josephine photographed,

we didn't even toy with a "do-it-yourself" proposition. After careful investigation, I found a man who was supposed to be marvelous with dogs. He arrived and overwhelmed me with his credits. He had photographed every well-known dog in Hollywood. He had just opened his studios in New York. As he explained it, those Hollywood dogs needed plenty of help. With his air brush he had taken away jowls, filled in scrawny tails, lengthened ears. There was nothing he couldn't do. He studied Josie and said he might do away with an inch or so of belly, but other than that, she was a natural.

Josie went off to the beauty parlor and arrived beribboned and beautiful for her sitting. I had no trouble teaching her how to pose. I merely showed her a "Yummy." She received it after the camera clicked. She got the idea after the third Yummy and was so enthusiastic about the whole setup, I think she secretly toyed with the idea of becoming a professional model. She sat, she turned, she stood, and she munched. I tell you, that dog would do anything for me—and a Yummy.

Even the photographer was captured by her charm. "She's the pos-i-tive end," he crooned. "Oh, she's going to be dee-vine. And I've solved the problem about her belly with su-perb lighting. And that face—girl, you are the end, the living end! Those ears! She should be in pictures. No dog I've ever photographed has such eyes. Oh, this is a real champ. I just must move in for a tighter closeup of that face—and those eyes. They're positively human. Darling, stop chewing that dreadful Yummy; it looks like sawdust. How CAN they like those things. All right, darling, open those mar-vel-ous eyes, open them, darling." (Darling's eyes were popping. She had never met anyone like this before.)

He rattled on. "I must send these pictures to *Vogue*. They'll go mad for her. Of course, they've been ple-ading with me to work for them, but I've refused. Darling, I'd go mad photographing those dreary looking girls. But photographing Josephine is the living end!"

He was still raving about Josie's face and photogenic qualities as he packed his equipment. This was music to my ears. I was mentally showing Bobo Eichenbaum's mother a full page picture of Josie in *Vogue*. Josie, along with all the other *slim* high-fashion models.

Naturally, when he asked me for a hundred dollar deposit, I sat down immediately and wrote the check. After all, as he explained, he was going to do some eight by ten blowups. Maybe he'd even offer them to *Life* for the cover. *Life* had been dying for his services for years.

Then he kissed me and Josie. "Well, much as I hate to leave you darlings, I must dash. You'll get the proofs in less than a week."

We watched him fly out the door. Josie hated to see him leave. He had taken at least seventy-five shots. And in her eyes, he represented seventy-five Yummies.

He kept his word about sending the proofs. They arrived five days later. I tore open the package. I stared in amazement. I couldn't believe my eyes. If I hadn't been right there, watching with my own eyes, I would have sworn that Irving had taken the shots. Seventy-five poses! Seventy-five ink blot tests! That's what it looked like. No eyes. No face. No teeth. No ears. Just a dense black outline. The close-ups looked like a giant Rorschach test.

I got on the phone and screamed. He screamed back. He said her coloring was all wrong for pictures. Brunettes were always rough, but she was such a brunette. Black eyes, black nose. . . .

I asked him what did he want me to do, paint her nose white and fit her with blue contact lenses?

That got to him. "Darling, what do you do with your hair to catch the light on television?"

"I spray gold powder on it."

"That's it! I'll be there immediately. We'll do the whole thing over. Rush out and buy masses of gold spray!"

I did. I also bought another box of Yummies. Josie was enchanted with the whole idea. She didn't even mind becoming a tipped blonde. In fact, she looked quite attractive. We went through seventy-five more prints and an equal amount of Yummies. He left promising me seventy-five thrilling studies. A week later they arrived. Seventy-five studies of a gold-tipped poodle with no eyes, no face, and no expression.

Not only did Irving tell off the photographer, but he also had a few choice things to say to me. Especially when we couldn't get the gold spray off Josie. And I thought he'd explode a few days later when the gold began to tarnish. Strangers stopped him on the street with "Hey Mister, your poodle is turning green," or "Look, Ma! What kind of a dog is that?"

I couldn't understand why we couldn't get it off. Even soap and water failed. I tried to tell Irving that when I used it, I just brushed it out of my hair with an ordinary hairbrush.

Irving refused to be placated. "Did it ever occur to you that possibly her hair might be different from yours? In fact, did it ever occur to you that she is an entity on her own? Equipped with *her* hair, *her* face, and her own personality?"

I was outraged. "What do you think I think?"

"That she's merely an extension of you! You like meat rare, she likes meat rare. Well, I happen to like meat well done. But I don't make her eat meat well done."

"What do you want me to do?

"Give her a chance to be herself. Maybe she likes her meat medium!"

I let him have the last word because secretly I had

to admit he had a point. Josie did have all of my characteristics and habits. She not only liked the same food, people, and television shows I liked, but she also shared my phobias. Take my fear of bugs, for example. I am not one of those shrinking females who shriek if a mouse enters a room. Personally, I think a mouse is very cute. But insects terrify me. Once in awhile one of those harmless summer moths flies into our apartment from the park. Now, most dogs, upon seeing a moth, happily dash after it—like "Tennis anyone?" But when a moth comes into our apartment, I rush into the bathroom in hysterics, and Josie dives under the bed until Irving makes like Frank Buck.

Irving says this is an outrageous situation. It's enough to have one nut like me on his hands. But poodles are born to be retrievers. They are born with the instinct to stalk big game—not flee for their lives from a moth!

There was no denying it. Irving was right. Suddenly I became acutely aware of the duality of our personalities. I love to eat in bed. Josie had gotten that message immediately. No matter where she was, if you tossed her a biscuit, she'd grab it, rush to the bedroom, and jump on the bed to eat it.

So I started a "Let-Josie-Be-Herself" campaign. In the past, whenever we took a walk, I automatically headed for Fifth Avenue, as I am an ardent window shopper. But with the new campaign, I let her make the decision. I stood in front of our hotel and said, "Where do you want to walk, Josephine?

For a moment she stared at me, then gave the leash a tug and automatically headed for Fifth Avenue.

I might have kept trying if I hadn't stumbled on an article in *Harper's Bazaar* or *Vogue*—or one of those magazines. (I was at the dentist's where I catch up on all my important reading.)

The article said, "Are Poodles People?"

Well, the idea behind the article is that some poodles are poodles. But some iconoclasts among the breed actually think they are people. (Of course, the few who think they are Great Danes we won't even discuss. They're sick!) But for the imaginative poodle who is positive he is a people, there is much to be said about the logic of his reasoning.

The article stated that some dogs have fur. But poodles do not. They have hair! Poodles use their paws like hands; they often cup a toy to play with it. Poodles wear winter coats, spring coats, rain coats, and hair ribbons. So why shouldn't a poodle, after surveying the human species and noting the similarities, automatically assume he is one of them?

I go along with that. If Josie and I go in the park on a rainy day, we wear mother and daughter trench coats. She not only sees me in a coat and herself in a coat, but she sees other *people* in trench coats. But the cocker spaniel she passed wasn't wearing one. Neither was the collie. So she decides she's definitely not a dog! Makes sense.

I went out and bought a few books on dog psychology. After much reading and inquiring around, I found there are certain tests you can make to find out whether your dog considers himself a poodle or a people.

Does he meet other poodles with wild enthusiasm and prefer their company to humans? Does he regard other breeds with normal interest? Does he understand a bark as well as your baby talk? If he does—you have a poodle.

Here are some of the symptoms of poodles who think they are people. They definitely prefer human companionship over any canine contemporary. To them, even Lassie is just a nice dog. Of all dogs, they favor the poodle. They regard other poodles with amused interest, as if to say, "My, that's a cute dog. If I ever had a pet, that's the kind I'd want."

The "Mirror Test" is the final and irrevocable answer. Because a positive characteristic of a poodle who is a people is the poodle's blind assumption that he looks exactly like his master.

To give the Mirror Test, you place poodle before a mirror. If it stares and preens, it is a poodle. If it stares and then slinks away, it is still a poodle—but it's a poodle in need of psychiatric help. Poodles are notoriously vain, and when a poodle doesn't enjoy preening, it shows he is not happy with himself. He might even be developing a "withdrawal complex." You must remedy this situation immediately by telling poodle on every possible occasion how beautiful he is. Also, a new beauty parlor and change of hair styling often gives poodle more confidence.

I gave Josephine the Mirror Test. She came through with a positive people reaction. She stared at herself for a moment. Then she turned to me with a quizzical look, as if to say, "Who does that cute dog belong to?"

Then, acting like people, she rushed over to pet the cute little dog. Naturally she got a resounding clump on the head from the mirror. That did it! She thought poodles were cute, but this was a nasty one. She growled. The dog growled back. She was furious. I had to grab her before she killed herself trying to attack this intruder.

The dog psychology book also says, "Make an effort to convince poodle he is a poodle. He will be easier to live with if you do."

I waited a few days and then tried a new approach with the Mirror Test. I held her in my arms and together we faced the mirror. I snuggled her against my face to give her security, and in a gentle voice said, "Josie, that is a mirror."

She stared at the affectionate tableau we presented. She seemed quite happy and even preened a bit. So far so good. I thought I had made my point, until I noticed that as she preened, she was looking at my reflection!

I decided to give her the unvarnished facts. I pointed

to our images. "Josephine, I hate to break this to you, but the little fat one with the Italian haircut is you. The tall, thin one is me."

She yawned, tossed the strange dog in the mirror a slight sneer, and returned her attention to the reflection of me. I gave up and never tried to convince her again. In a way, I was flattered that she had decided to look like me. She could have chosen Irving.

16

Smile!
You're on Camera!

OF COURSE, it had to happen. With everyone in the family connected with television, Josephine just naturally fell into the life. Experts claim average dogs understand five or six words or commands. Smart dogs understand twenty to thirty words—like cooky, walk, dinner, Daddy, Mommy, icebox, haircut(!), Yummies, NO, good boy, etc. Josie not only knew all these old standards, but her knowledge even extended to words like sponsors, Nielsons, shares, prime time, tape, summer replacement, and pilot film. She knew that "cancellation" was a four letter word and that "option time" meant stomach trouble. She knew the word "thirteen" was not just a number, but a television cycle. Twenty-six meant a good television cycle, and thirty-nine meant, "Throw away the Miltown, we're in."

Her belly had been rubbed by Milton Berle, Jack E. Leonard, Clifton Fadiman, Earl Wilson, Ed Sullivan, Keefe Brasselle, and her godfather, that famous teetotaler, Joe E. Lewis. In fact, her belly had been rubbed by so many "name" hands, it could be compared to the cement in front of Grauman's Chinese Theater where all the Hollywood Greats put their footprints. It was almost getting to the point where you could point to Josie's belly and say, "Lucille Ball was there last night!"

Of course people didn't just walk into our apartment and exclaim, "Where's Josephine's belly? I want to rub it." It was something they wound up doing in spite of themselves. Half the time people rubbed her belly without even realizing it. Josephine engineered the whole process.

The moment anyone arrived, Josephine took over as a one man reception committee. She cooed, she jumped, she danced around them like a regular Kathryn Murray. Personally, I thought she came on a little too strong with this welcome bit, yet it never failed. Everyone was always flattered. After all, how was one to know she gave the window cleaner and the grocery boy the same effusive greeting. Wherever the guest sat, Josephine was Johnny-on-the-spot, snuggling right beside him. If he was a normal, healthy extrovert, he automatically scratched the top of her head. If he wasn't imaginative enough to do this on his own, she'd promote the idea with the "paw bit." The paw bit was a gentle scratch on the arm with her paw. If this was ignored, it came on stronger. (As Bea Cole once remarked, "My God! here she comes again with that shiv paw!") So you can see why it was easier to scratch her than to ignore her. Most people scratched away as they talked. Once this routine was set in a steady, unconscious motion, Josephine got into position and with the shiv paw nudged their hands to the desired spot—the great white belly. And that's how it went. If they even stopped to light a cigarette, they received a gentle jab from the shiv paw.

Josie's biggest windfall of belly rubbers came when Irving held auditions at our apartment. Most of his auditions were confined to the television studio or his office, but there were times when evening appointments were necessary. Then a steady stream of ambitious young performers streamed through our door. Now, if you were an ambitious young performer wanting to get on "Talent Scouts" and a fat little black poodle who belonged to the producer demanded that you rub its belly, what would you do? You'd do what any normal talented young performer would do. You'd rub its belly as if this were your real mission in life.

So you can see that it was a natural for Josie, basking in this atmosphere of love and affection, to grow into a very adjusted but theatrically inclined girl poodle. It figured for her to go into the business.

At first I made no active move to get her career rolling. I figured she'd be discovered eventually. Can anyone forget the thrilling story of how Mervyn LeRoy discovered Lana Turner sipping a coke in a drugstore? How Norma Shearer saw that darling picture of little Janet Leigh on Janet's mother's desk in a hunting lodge? These things happen. Only they didn't happen to Josephine.

And plenty of important people saw her, but they just weren't in the discovering mood. Billy Rose never batted an imaginative eyelash in her direction. Of course this didn't really bother me, because Billy still kids about the time a young unknown named Mary Martin auditioned for him and he told her to go back to Texas, get married, and have babies. Besides, Billy was only producing theaters, mansions, and millions these days. Abe Burrows was perfectly willing to rub her belly, but it never crossed his mind to use her in one of his musicals. My good friend Earl Wilson who writes reams about amply endowed girls like Jane Russell, Monique Van Vooren, Jayne Mansfield, and even unknown chesty beauties, never devoted any space to Josie. And Josie is not only beautiful, she's more than amply endowed—she has ten of them! Even Sidney Kingsley, her old buddy, remained strangely aloof in regard to her entry into show business.

In a way, it was Anna Sosenko who got the whole thing going. Anna is a woman of many talents. She wrote "Darling, Je Vous Aime Beaucoup," discovered Hildegarde, and is a great expert on art. But Josie

loved Anna for herself. Anna was an indefatigable
belly rubber, and Anna also had a lovely terrace with
an electric grill that made hot dogs. And Anna always
had little goodies like caviar or *pâté* canapés hanging
around.

One day Anna, Josie, and I were sitting around
doing nothing in particular on Anna's terrace. That
is, Josie and I were doing nothing in particular. Anna
was quite busy. She was mixing martinis with one
hand and rubbing Josie's belly with the other. Suddenly this tranquil scene was interrupted—a news-
paperman Anna knew dropped by to pay an unexpected
visit. Naturally, Anna was delighted to see him. I was
impressed with meeting him, as I had read his articles,
but to Josephine, he meant only one thing—a new
sucker! Besides, if she released Anna, it would give
Anna some time to whip up those marvelous canapés.
So she rushed to greet this man as if he were a blood
relative. Naturally, the man, who had never met
either of us, was extremely flattered.

And naturally, I came up with the stock statement
that rarely fails, "My, I've never seen her act like this.
She really seems to like you."

It didn't fail because he answered on cue, "I don't
know what it is, but all dogs just seem to take to me."

I stared at him with proper awe. "They must. She
doesn't take to strangers." (She'd take to Khrushchev
if he greeted her with a piece of liverwurst and a free
right hand.)

And when Josie hit him up for some belly rubbing,
even Anna got the idea and began to come out with
the right little phrases. "Oh, she wants you to rub her
tummy. She only lets people she adores do that."

When he stopped rubbing to accept a drink, Josie
gave him the shiv paw as a gentle reminder of his real
mission in life.

Instead of being annoyed, he was enchanted. "She
actually communicates!"

Well, even I had to admit this was a new word for

being clawed to death. I began to adore this man. Before long we were discussing the possibilities of Josephine's embarking on a theatrical career. He insisted he would take care of it. His parting words were, "I know a man at NBC."

I didn't take it too seriously because *everyone* knows "a man at NBC," but I did give him our phone number and expressed our willingness to listen to any worthwhile offer.

Irving was against the idea at first. Why should she have to bother with TV? If I got my kicks from being stabbed or shot on "Studio One" and "Suspense," that was up to me. But Josie didn't seem to need any outlet for her self-expression.

But I was determined. I wanted her to realize there was more to life than playing catch, eating Yummies, and having her belly rubbed. Besides, she could help the breed. Too many people thought of poodles as arrogant little lap dogs and nothing more. I was tired of hearing the usual clichés: "Oh, poodles are all right if you want a silly, fussy dog to dress up and attract attention with, but give me a real dog." Or "A mutt is the smartest dog. All those purebreds have very low IQs."

Also, since the "Jackie Coogan law," Josie could be sure that I wouldn't use any of her hard-earned money for my own personal luxuries. Her money would all go into AT&T. She could use the dividends for Yummies or special chewing toys. And if she really caught on and became a star, she could hire a personal belly rubber by the hour.

My friends agreed that Josie should be on TV. Especially when they heard how she would use the AT&T dividends. We all sat and waited for the call from the man who knew a man at NBC.

We didn't get the call. But we did get a letter. Unfortunately, our benefactor was being sent by his newspaper to cover some uprising in India, Africa, or China, or one of those places that always has a small war going on. But he hadn't forgotten Josephine. He would attend to her career as soon as he returned.

I was very depressed because those small wars go on forever. As far as wars go, if there has to be one, give me a good major out-in-the-open war anytime. Everyone knows about them, and everyone does something about it to get them finished. But it's those sneaky little wars you have to watch out for. Where you read on page two that some terrorists have killed four people on a side street and strafed an office building. I never know whom we're rooting for—the terrorists or the four people on the side street. And no one seems to really do anything about them, except maybe make a few speeches at the U.N., and sometimes some country sends them some money and a few outmoded fighter planes. Only this time they sent Josie's television contract.

I sat and sulked a few days until Anna Sosenko fired me into action. "If you want her to have a career, do something about it!"

"Like what?"

"Like letting the word get around that Josie is available. After all, when people see her taking a stroll with you, they just see a poodle. They don't realize she's a talent." Then Anna paused for a moment. "By the way, what does she do?"

"She doesn't do anything special, she's just a natural."

Anna stared as Josie devoured the piece of sturgeon she offered her. "To me, she looks like a natural born slob!"

That did it! I had to show Anna. I called everyone and within one week Josie got an offer. I knew a girl whose mother worked for the ASPCA. The ASPCA had a segment of the Herb Sheldon show. A few words were spoken in the right places, and suddenly I received a call from a man from NBC. Would Josie appear on the Herb Sheldon show the following week?

"Doing what?" (You see, you mustn't sound too anxious.)

"Well, Mr. Sheldon makes a small speech about the ASPCA and all the good it does. Then he will introduce you, and you can introduce Josephine and say a few words about how a pet brightens your life. Naturally, while you speak, the camera will come in close on Josephine." (So she got all the closeups! I refused to let that bother me. This was *her* debut, not mine!)

I kept my voice filled with enthusiasm. "And what will you pay her?"

"Oh, there's no salary connected with the appearance."

My enthusiasm began to wane. No closeups for me. No money for her! "But she's a member of AFTRA," I lied.

"That's all right. AFTRA recognizes all charitable agencies and allows free appearances to help their causes."

"But what about me? I have to go on with her."

"Now we mustn't think of it that way, Miss Susann. We must think of you as being sort of a glorified prop for Josephine."

"A prop?"

"That's right. The ASPCA doesn't feature people, it features animals. Now, we'll expect you both next Thursday at eight-thirty in the morning." Eight-thirty in the morning!

I immediately launched into a lengthy detailed explanation of the sleeping and living habits of the Mansfields, including Josephine, which, when boiled down, amounted to: "Get some other dog."

He got the message and hung up.

Ten minutes later Irving phoned. The man from NBC had gotten to him and Irving had agreed that for such a worthwhile organization as the ASPCA Josephine would certainly appear, in spite of the early hour. "After all," he said, "it is a good cause."

"Then if you're so big suddenly with the causes, you take her on!"

I could almost hear him smirk on the phone: "*I*

didn't go around opening my big mouth, trying to get her on TV."

I raved on and on. Didn't he have any consideration for her? He knew she hated to get up before noon. And even if she did manage to pull herself together, I couldn't! What about my career? How would I look facing the TV cameras at such an ungodly hour?

His next remark ended the entire discussion. "Who is even going to look at *you* when *she* is on camera at the same time?"

So Josephine went to the beauty parlor for the ten-dollar session, and I washed and set my own hair. The night before the show, I turned out the lights at ten o'clock and left a call for seven in the morning. At twelve, I was still wide awake and Josie was playing with a squeak toy in the living room. I marched in, grabbed her, and snuggled her in bed with me. I explained we had to go to sleep—immediately! (Irving was holed up in the den reading.)

Josie was perfectly content to snuggle, except that she kept giving me the shiv paw. Finally she got the idea. For some crazy reason she was expected to stay in bed with me. I must say she accepted it gracefully. She went out and brought all of her toys into the bed. For hours she crunched away on her prepared toy bone. She lunged at the loudest squeak toy, she brought a wet ball and placed it right on my face. It really wasn't her fault. To her, one A.M. was the shank of the evening. At two A.M. I took a sleeping pill and gave her half an aspirin and a few drops of whiskey. We both slept fairly well after that.

The next morning she looked marvelous and was full of pep. I looked dreadful and felt hung-over from the pill. But together, we trekked to NBC. Irving had already alerted all of his friends. His mother had alerted half of Brooklyn. Anna Sosenko, who never sleeps, was going to tape record the entire performance. Friends of ours in North Bergen, Judge Rosenblum and his wife Fran, were taking care of the New Jersey area. Bea Cole had aroused all of upper Park Avenue, and Karen alerted her first-grade class. Joyce had set her alarm for eight thirty. She, Vicki, and Toulouse were going to watch. Joyce's mother had prepped Huntington, Long Island. In all respect to Mr. Herb Sheldon, you can see he was a very fortunate man. This girl carried her own do-it-yourself Trendex.

Everyone was very nice to us at the studio. No actual rehearsal was required. Just a lighting run-through, so they could look at the "star" on camera and adjust the lights. I held her while men climbed to the ceiling and added dimmers and hot whites. They really went all out! "Put in a scoop, Pete, I want to catch her eyes." "Give me a floorlight, it will high-light her nose." (I never got half this attention when I starred on "Studio One." But Josie took it all with a bored yawn.)

In fact, she was so lethargic about the whole thing that I began to worry whether her dazzling personal-ity would come through. After all, she wasn't used to the early morning hours. She was a "night person." She might come over as just a lump. This thought had never occurred to me. I put her on the floor and tried to interest her in a game of tag. She curled up and immediately went to sleep. I was hysterical. It *was* too early in the morning for her!

The director stared. "She will come to life when the show starts, won't she?"

I nodded with an assurance I did not feel. Suddenly it was nine o'clock . . . everyone went tense . . . the theme began . . . the show was on the air!

Five minutes later, Josie and I were introduced. There are some performers who are marvelous at dress rehearsals but freeze when the camera goes on or when they face a live audience. Then there are performers who feel nothing until they face an audience. Then they spark, they're inspired, their whole personality

changes, they become "bigger than life." The trade
calls them "naturals" or born performers. Josie was a
natural.

The moment we were introduced and the cameras
moved in, she came alive. She opened those gorgeous
eyes and oozed personality. She cocked her head at
her best angle. As the camera inched in for a tight
closeup, the actor in me came to the front. So far it
had been her show all the way. But it wouldn't hurt if
I got in the act. I snuggled her against my face. This
way we'd both have stunning closeups. (That's what
I thought!)

I hadn't counted on Josie's suddenly turning into a
regular Ethel Barrymore. Josie shares the spotlight
with no one! As the camera moved in on this charming
mother-daughter closeup, daughter suddenly sprang
into action and decided to cover Mummy's face with
loving little kisses. This was a tender scene, except that
Mummy's face suddenly was obliterated from the
picture. The director, thrilled with this ad lib piece
of business, quickly called for camera two, to take the
shot from the rear. This caught Josie full face plus
a stunning view of the back of my head.

Naturally, she was an unqualified hit. NBC's switchboard lit up with calls about her. Was her name Josephine or Josie? What was her real name before she
went on television? How old was she? How many
puppies did she have? You know, all the important
things people want to know about celebrities. No one
called about me.

And when we got home, my phone never stopped.
Joyce said she made a bum out of Lassie. Mrs. Eichenbaum said even her belly didn't show. Irving said Josie
had proven beyond a doubt that brunettes do photo-
graph on TV. However, in the one fleeting glimpse
he had gotten of me, I had looked pretty bad!

"Bad like how?" I inquired.

"Oh nothing serious. Just kind of washed out."

Naturally. I had been using *her* lighting. How could I look good in black poodle lighting? It was a wonder I was seen at all. I spent the rest of the day taking congratulatory calls for Josephine.

Late that night, just as Irving was dozing off, I said, "Irving, just how washed out did I look?"

He yawned. "Real washed out. Good night. I love you."

I was suddenly genuinely alarmed. "Irving! Maybe it will hurt my career."

"That's ridiculous."

"Why is it ridiculous?"

He yawned again. "Because you looked so lousy, no one will ever believe it was you. Now stop talking and go to sleep!"

I stopped talking. But I didn't sleep!

17

Return Engagement

THE FOLLOWING DAY NBC called. They wanted Josephine back for a return engagement. As a rule, they never repeated a guest, but Josephine had been such a smash, they were willing to make an exception.

I agreed. After all, my pride in her innate showmanship overcame any personal vanity.

Irving seemed concerned. "What are you going to do about your looks in her lights?"

"We'll compromise. I'll have them toned down. She won't look quite as gorgeous and I won't look quite as gruesome."

Irving said there was a better way to effect a compromise.

"Like how?"

"Like buying a reflector and sitting in the sun for an hour every day. You've got a whole week to catch up to her."

So I sat in the park and tanned and planned. How was Josie going to top last week's appearance? She couldn't just return, give them the same dazzling smile, and let it go at that. To be a star, you've got to score each time at bat. After all, it takes more than one home run to make a Mantle or a Maris. Ed Sullivan presents a different star every week. And even Jack Paar attacks a new country or columnist on each performance.

Josie had to do something different this week. Unfortunately, Josie had done everything she knew how to do last week.

Well, it was now up to me. She needed a gimmick . . . a trick . . . or a stooge. A stooge! Bobo Eichenbaum!

I asked Mrs Eichenbaum if Bobo would like to go on television. Would Bobo like to go on television! Mrs. Eichenbaum began to quiver with delight. He'd do anything! He'd be so thrilled just to be a part of show biz. It didn't matter how menial—Bobo on television! No one in the Eichenbaum family had ever been on the stage! And for Bobo to start in such a major way—on television—on NBC!

I explained that it was Josie who would appear. Bobo would just kind of be a walk-on. It didn't matter to the breathless Mrs. Eichenbaum. He'd do *anything!* Just tell her what he had to do—in preparation.

I said he was to take a good long walk in the park just before he went on camera. Then he was to do nothing! I didn't know how long they'd allow us on camera, last time it was just two minutes. But if I had time, I'd even mention his name.

Mention his name! Mrs. Eichenbaum swooned. What a thrill! She'd get to hear me say "Bobo" over the television!

That's how it went on Wednesday. On Thursday she was less breathless but more practical. What should Bobo wear? His black sequined collar or his red kid sport collar with the little rhinestone initials?

He was to wear a plain collar. Any stones caused halations. (Of course, I had to do ten minutes on "what were halations?" In the end she still refused to believe Perry Como or Garry Moore wore blue shirts. On her set they were white.)

On Friday, Mrs. Eichenbaum had some new questions. Did the program go to Miami? She had relatives there. Should Bobo go to the beauty parlor a day before the show or was there a hairdresser on the set?

Well, I couldn't swear for the station lineup, but I

could vouch that this particular NBC show emanated from a small studio on West Sixty-seventh Street and in no way resembled the studios of Metro-Goldwyn-Mayer. Bobo would have to do his own hair.

What about Chicago? Mr. Eichenbaum knew a lot of people in Chicago. I began to get embarrassed when I couldn't even promise her Chicago. Somewhere I had a sneaky feeling this was a local show. So you can imagine how happy I was when she got around to Paterson, New Jersey. I guaranteed her Paterson!

Saturday and Sunday passed uneventfully. (I had gone to Philadelphia to visit my mother.) But Monday was chock full of activity! It was twenty-four hours until showtime!

The first call from Mrs. Eichenbaum came at noon. And it was a bone crusher. What should she wear? I tried to remain calm even though I sensed catastrophe could follow.

"Wear? What do you mean?"

"Well, I don't want to cause halations. Does a print halate?"

"Hattie," I said tenderly (that was Mrs. Eichenbaum's personal handle), "you can wear anything. It's Bobo who is going on."

There was a deathlike pause. Finally, "And how does Bobo get on?"

"You place him on the floor and give him a shove."

Another interminable pause. Then: "But why should he get shoved on when he could be carried on with dignity?"

"Because that's the way it's got to be. When Bobo comes on, the camera will pan down to the floor, and *I* won't even be seen. Just the two dogs. Besides, with the lighting they give the dogs, only a black dog can look good. You're a glorious redhead, Hattie dear, you'd completely fade out. I'm a brunette, and even I didn't look very well in those lights."

"Oh, is that why you looked so bad?" Then after

a thoughtful pause, "But look, I don't care how bad I look. Just so they see me. After all, I want everyone in Paterson, New Jersey to believe it's really Bobo. And they won't believe it unless they see me carry him on."

"But I'll say his name is Bobo."

"That won't convince Paterson. Bobo is a very popular name for a poodle. There are two Bobos who live at the Essex House. One at the Hampshire House. There are three Bobos on Fifty-Seventh Street. And my sister knows a Bobo in Paterson who isn't even a poodle."

I saw her point. "Okay, Hattie, I'll announce him as Bobo Eichenbaum. And don't you dare tell me there is more than one Bobo Eichenbaum running around!"

Two hours later Mrs. Eichenbaum was back on the phone. "He's at the beauty parlor now. Any special way you think he should be trimmed to make him stand out more?"

"Don't change a hair on his head. Just let him appear as he really is, and I assure you, his true charm will come across."

"But I don't want him to look like just another poodle."

I could see it was time for me to be firm. "Mrs. Eichenbaum, I can always get another poodle to go on with Josie. But can Bobo get another television show?"

Mrs. Eichenbaum got the message. "Okay, nothing fancy." Those were her parting words.

But when we met in the hotel lobby at eight the following morning, it was obvious that Mrs. Eichenbaum had not lived up to her contract. Bobo was brushed and scrubbed to an inch of his life. He also sported large beautiful satin hair ribbons on his ears.

I looked at Bobo, then at Mrs. Eichenbaum. I pointed to his ears. "The bows must go!"

Mrs. Eichenbaum feigned amazement. "Why? Josephine is wearing yellow bows and yellow nail polish."

I said, "When Bobo has his own show he can wear yellow bows and nail polish."

Mrs. Eichenbaum stood firm. Didn't Josie want her supporting cast to look good? After all, it reflected on her, didn't it? A star was only as good as the cast around him. I stared at Mrs. Eichenbaum. For a woman so far removed from show business, she had suddenly turned into a regular David Belasco.

I reiterated. "No bows for Bobo."

Mrs. Eichenbaum began to pout. This was just what I needed at eight-fifteen in the morning—to stand around in a hotel lobby and fight the battle of the bows.

I started for the door. "Are you coming?"

Bobo started to follow, but Mrs. Eichenbaum refused to budge. "And if I refuse to take off the bows. Then what?

"Then there will be a lot of disappointed people in Paterson, New Jersey."

Paterson, New Jersey, proved to be the magic words. At least they brought Mrs. Eichenbaum back to reality and her relatives. She leaned down and removed the bows. Secretly, I felt like a heel. The bows definitely did something for Bobo. But that's how it is in the jungle of show biz—you have to protect the star!

Mrs. Eichenbaum is essentially a very good-natured woman. By the time we reached the studio, the bows were an incident of the past and she was bouncing with anticipation. When she saw the cameras and crew, she went numb with excitement; when the director and crew saw two poodles, they also went a little numb.

Someone from the staff rushed over to take charge. "I'm awfully sorry, Miss Susann, but we have no studio audience. Your friend and her dog will have to leave."

Mrs. Eichenbaum suddenly came to life. "What dog? He's an actor."

I quickly made the necessary introductions and explanations. Just as quickly, an immediate conference was called among the show's personnel. The director returned. Could he see a rehearsal of this "act." No, he could not. A rehearsal would take away the spontaneity. Josephine had to feel things—she was a method actress.

He returned to his group. There was another huddled conference. The director came back with a counter offer. Would I mind giving him a verbal rundown of the "act"? It wasn't that Herb Sheldon doubted my unerring good taste or theatrical instinct. He always got that worried look whenever he saw more than one dog at a time. And the director wasn't worried either. It was just the usual red tape. Things like this had to be cleared at the front office.

I gave him the rundown. Herb Sheldon would introduce me and Josie. The camera could close in on Josie, and at the same time I'd make a pitch for the ASPCA, explaining it was Josie's favorite organization. Then I'd explain about Josie's friend, Bobo. His love and devotion for her. I'd put Josie on the floor—that would be the cue for a camera to pan to the ground. At the same time, it would be the floor manager's business to give Mrs. Eichenbaum a hand cue to put Bobo on the floor. (She would be standing off camera holding Bobo.) Once she released him, naturally, he'd come straight to Josie. He'd get on his hind legs to embrace her. She'd respond.

The director said it was a beautiful plot. It really got him—and he hated to be such a stickler for details—but could he just see this marvelous pantomime. After all, he wanted to time it, so he could see how much he'd have to cut out of the rest of the show. It wasn't that he was a killjoy, but the ASPCA had only told him to expect a two-minute bit, and the way he saw it, at least two of Mr. Sheldon's monologues would have to go.

I said I would make my opening pitch short and

that I was positive we could bring in the spot in four minutes. Being a director of unusual daring and courage, he gave me a sickly grin and went off to tell Mr. Sheldon the thrilling news.

The show began. We went on and Josie was her usual scintillating self. That same magic appeared simultaneously with the red light of the camera. As I delivered my speech for the ASPCA, Josie turned and gave me a small kiss on the nose. Just as I was about to place her on the floor, she turned and touched my pearls. Now I swear she had seen those pearls a hundred times, but suddenly she acted like Jules Glaenzer of Cartier's. (She couldn't have cared less about the pearls, but she did know she was right in the middle of a closeup and she was in no rush to go to the floor and share a two-shot with Bobo.)

I got the message immediately and co-operated with her. She studied my pearls as if she had a jeweler's glass, I took them off and put them on her neck. She preened. They did look stunning. After all, there's nothing like pearls on basic black. Finally, I removed them and put her on the floor. The A.D. tapped the ever-patient Mrs. Eichenbaum on the shoulder. She put Bobo on the floor and pointed him in Josie's direction. Bobo saw Josie and started toward her—then he saw the camera! He stopped dead, turned and rushed back to Mrs. Eichenbaum. (Naturally, the camera recorded none of this offstage tableau. It merely remained on Josie, who sat poised and amused at Bobo's stage fright.)

Mrs. Eichenbaum gently but firmly placed Bobo toward Josie again and gave him a gentle shove. He stared at Josie, then at the cameras, then at Josie—and love overcame all. He was drawn toward this siren in spite of his fright of the unknown. As he drew into camera range and close to Josie, the alien atmosphere dissolved. He forgot the heat of the lights, the strange men, the cameras. All he saw was the Liz Taylor of the poodle world. He approached her with lovelight actually dripping from his eyes. And Josie, who realized the agony he was enduring, extended herself. She stood on her hind legs to greet him. Naturally, he leaped into her arms. She allowed him to hold her longer than usual and didn't even grimace when he grew bold enough to kiss her on the nose. (You can see what an actress she is, because Bobo is just not her type, and the kiss had been strictly an ad lib on his part.)

Finally, when she had had it, she gently released Bobo and dismissed him by turning her back. On cue, Bobo stood on his hind legs and waved his paws, begging for her attention. Naturally, they were a sensation.

The director said he never would have believed that two poodles could sustain a ten-minute spot. All the stagehands congratulated Josephine. Bobo came in for his share of applause. For an amateur, he had come through with flying colors.

But Bobo wasn't interested in any praise. Josie had kissed him. He kept his adoring eyes glued to her pompous little figure. As we left the studio, he went to nuzzle her. She turned and growled her displeasure. He attempted to sneak another kiss and she snapped at him.

"Poor Bobo," Mrs. Eichenbaum said sadly. "He doesn't realize she was only acting. He didn't know he was on television. He thought they were actually playing a love scene."

I was glad that Mrs. Eichenbaum understood. It was true. Bobo had no idea he had been on camera. As he walked down the hall, he pranced ahead, eager for the next adventure in life—whether it be a kiss from Josie or a walk in the park. He was really a very nice, uncomplicated dog. But Josephine, like all great actresses, was drained after a performance. She had thought up exciting little pieces of business on her own—like the pearl bit—and she had submitted to Bobo's unexpected amorous advances. Her nerves were really frayed. So, as we walked down the hall at NBC, she suddenly displayed a slight burst of temperament. She squatted! Right on the nice, shiny NBC floor.

Mrs. Eichenbaum and Bobo ran away as if they didn't know us. I played it cool. I never changed my gait and strolled nonchalantly down the corridor with Josie, as if to say: "Doesn't everyone use the hall of NBC as a powder room?"

Mrs. Eichenbaum wouldn't have been human if she hadn't pointed with great pride at Bobo's performing at the first fire hydrant we ran into. In fact, all the way home she asked guarded little questions like: "Who at MCA booked poodles? Was William Morris or GAC better for television guest shots?" She felt maybe Bobo did have a theatrical career on his horizon. After all, he didn't have an accident in the hallway at NBC.

But Mrs. Eichenbaum dropped the idea immediately. It seems that, when Bobo got home, he had what you might term a delayed reaction. He vomited for two days.

18

Grandma

Josie's television debut with Herb Sheldon occurred during the late spring of 1955. She received several offers from other television shows, but Irving refused to let her work during the summer. As he put it, toiling under the hot TV lights in the summer was too strenuous for a little girl poodle who was only a year and a half old. So I explained to everyone that Josie was "on vacation."

We remained in New York for the summer. Irving was putting together a new television show and Josie and I just loafed. Toward the end of the summer, Irving longed for two weeks of golf at the Concord.

We called Lorraine Trydell and Ray Parker who ran this vast establishment and asked if dogs were allowed. "Frenchy" as Miss Trydell is called, said they didn't encourage this kind of patronage, but they did make exceptions. So on a lovely day in August, Irving, "the exception," and I drove to the Concord at Kiamesha Lake. I love the Concord. The golf course is sensational, the food is great, and the bedrooms are unbelievable. We had one that boasted "His" and "Her" bathrooms, indirect lighting, a television set— the luxury of the Waldorf in the mountains. Everyone who visits the Concord for the first time is overwhelmed. Everyone but Josephine.

From the very beginning she took a dim view of the entire move. She watched the doorman at our hotel help us load our car with luggage and golf bags. She got a wild look when she saw her box of toys and Yummies join the assemblage. And an even wilder look when she realized she was to be part of this caravan.

I drove, and Irving held her in his lap. But she refused to relax. She barked at every toll booth, she refused to nap, she didn't even enjoy belly rubbing. She felt it was her duty to remain alert and awake. She was suspicious about the whole thing and she intended to find out what was going on!

Even the large bedroom with the two bathrooms failed to impress her. She made it plain that she had no desire to stay. After sniffing every corner of the room, she headed for the door, and gave us a flip wag of her tail, which meant, "All right, now let's get the hell out of here!"

To show her displeasure, she refused to eat. And anyone who won't eat the food served at the Concord is really disturbed. I couldn't get it through her head that this was just a temporary move—a vacation. She figured we had moved permanently, and she missed everything near and dear to her—Central Park, Fifth Avenue, shopping expeditions to Bloomingdale's. Let's face it, she was a city dog, and all the fresh mountain air got on her nerves. Besides, she didn't play golf, she didn't swim, and when I took her for a walk, there wasn't even anything interesting to sniff. Just clean mountain grass.

We had a wonderful time, and I hated to leave at the end of two weeks. But Josephine's whole personality changed the moment she saw our bags being loaded into the car. And when we finally hit the West Side highway, she was a new girl. When we drove down Central Park South, she almost choked with delight. She was home!

She kissed our doorman. She kissed all the bellboys —even the one she didn't like. She rolled on the carpeted floor of the lobby. Who needed fresh mountain grass? She was happier rolling on broadloom. Irving and I felt very bad about the whole thing. Josephine was a dyed-in-the-wool New Yorker. She'd never be happy away from the city.

And oh how Josephine loved autumn in New York. But winter was a little different. Each day she'd prance out, expecting to find the temperature the same as in our apartment. When the cold air hit her, she'd stop in amazement. Then, being an extremely practical dog, she'd attend to the business at hand and drag us back to the hotel. No brisk invigorating walks for her! She was content to get her exercise in a steam-heated apartment.

In January, Josie celebrated her second birthday. In February she made her first network television appearance on the Robert Q. Lewis show. This time congratulations poured in on an even larger scale. Friends in Los Angeles saw her. So did Irving's cousin in Detroit. And most important, my mother, in Philadelphia saw her. And my mother, who by nature is most reticent, took bows all over town.

She had accepted the title of Grandma without a murmur—my mother is a born "animal nut"—although she lives without a dog or cat.

My mother has a brand-new gold broadloom rug! And if Dr. Ben Casey (who my mother thinks is just adorable) happened to drop by for tea, my mother would make him remove his shoes before he set foot on her gold broadloom rug.

She also has hard luck with pets. Take the tank of beautiful tropical fish she had. Now some people buy a few fish and wind up with millons of shimmering beauties. But my mother bought a million fish and wound up with cannibals. No matter what she fed them, they preferred eating one another. This went on until she wound up with a big tank and one fat victorious murderer. Naturally her heart wasn't bursting with love for this three-inch monster who had devoured all of his relatives and neighbors, but an innate softheartedness kept her from letting him starve to death. She bought all kinds of fancy fish food, which he rejected. He lost weight but stubbornly refused the food. My mother was just as stubborn. She wasn't going to get him a living human fish to eat. That would be criminal. It became a battle of temperaments. Who would give in first? The fish won. He died of starvation. In a way it was for the best. Mother was just about to give in. She had already made inquiries about inexpensive live goldfish.

Then there was the canary who wouldn't sing. And the two love birds who despised each other. They sat at opposite sides of the cage and glared at one another. Then one of them died. Now it's a known fact that when one love bird dies, the other automatically follows within twenty-four hours. But not Mother's love birds! The remaining love bird suddenly became a living doll. It grew new feathers and chirped its head off all day long. It finally died three years later of a throat hemorrhage from so much singing and happiness.

But Irving's mother presented a different kind of problem. She was also a widow and lived alone—without an animal to her name. And she didn't have a gold broadloom rug. She just didn't like animals. However she was a very reasonable woman, and since Irving and I had gone so loony about Josephine, she effected a compromise. Although she drew the line about accepting Josie as a blood relative, she promised to regard her as a friend of the family.

But show business is the great equalizer. Remember how Princess Margaret befriended Danny Kaye? And if Grace Kelly hadn't won that Oscar and starred in all those movies, how would Prince Rainier have ever discovered her? Well, why should my mother-in-law be less impressionable than Princess Margaret or Prince Rainier? She suddenly became much more affable toward Josephine after Josie's TV appearances. I noticed this when I brought Josie to Brooklyn for a visit. Just from her introduction alone. She said,

"Jackie, you know my friend Mrs. Braff, and Mrs. Braff this is Josephine our poodle from the Herb Sheldon and Robert Q. Lewis show."

But that spring I noticed she didn't have her usual energy. Naturally she insisted that she felt fine, but after careful interrogation, I learned that my mother-in-law had not been to a doctor since Irving was born. Her theory was when you got so sick that you couldn't get out of bed, then you got up and went to see a doctor! Otherwise it was just looking for trouble.

I insisted that she come to New York and stay with us, and have a complete physical checkup. Naturally she refused. We won out by putting it on a personal basis. We merely threatened never to come to Brooklyn and let her cook those eleven-course meals for us unless she came and spent a few weeks at our house and took some tests on the side. Naturally on these terms, she had to accept. No one was more delighted about her visit than Josephine. This meant captive company all day long.

As I have stated, Josie knows many words. I taught them all to my mother-in-law: "Get your ball!" "Sit up!" "Lie down!" "Let's take a walk!" and then the most important: "I'm busy!" When Josie hears those two words, she heaves a sigh but obediently turns her attention to another person or a toy. I told my mother-in-law not to hesitate to use those words whenever Josie's adoration became too cloying.

Nevertheless I'd invariably come home and find Josie lying on the couch, her head in my mother-in-law's lap, while that good woman rubbed Josie's belly with such diligence you'd swear she was getting paid by the hour.

I'd say, "Mom, isn't this the time you usually watch 'Secret Storm' or 'Young Doctor Malone'?" (She adored soap operas.)

She'd nod and say, "But if I got up to turn on the set I'd disturb her."

I'd try to reason with her. "Mom, you're in New

York. There's so much to see. You're here to enjoy yourself, not to be Josephine's companion and belly rubber."

My mother-in-law gave me a wistful smile and continued with the rubbing. "But she enjoys my company."

At the same time Josie tossed me an indignant glance that plainly stated, "Are *we* bothering you? Keep your big mouth shut!"

"But you can watch television and she can still enjoy your company," I argued. "You can even read a book or take a walk together." Then I went on to explain about the wonders of Radio City Music Hall, the thrilling sales in all the department stores, the marvels of the great outside world that was awaiting her. Somehow Josephine would manage to stumble through a day without six hours of belly rubbing.

My mother-in-law nodded in agreement but continued with the rubbing. "But she enjoys it so much."

I stared at the two of them, and suddenly it seemed that the expanse of Josie's great white belly had taken on even more magnificent proportions. Maybe all the rubbing had stretched it!

Later on I watched Josie waddle across the room. Suddenly I knew I wasn't imagining things. Her belly was larger! I asked my mother-in-law if she had been slipping Josie any extra Yummies.

She was indignant! She *never* gave Josie Yummies. She didn't believe in feeding anyone between meals. Besides, she had tasted one of those Yummies just to find out what was in them. They weren't fit for a dog! The man who called them dog candy must have been a dog catcher. They tasted like frozen sawdust.

I explained that dogs like the taste. To Josie it was candy.

My mother-in-law shook her head. "She just pretends to—to please you. She has a very sweet nature."

I stared at Josie. Well, maybe it was just my imagination, but her belly did look larger. I put her on the scale. It wasn't my imagination. Josie had picked up two extra pounds.

Naturally I phoned the vet for an immediate appointment. My mother-in-law insisted she was living with a bunch of hypochondriacs! There she had been, sitting in Brooklyn, minding her own business, and we rushed her to New York because she had lost a few pounds. Now we were rushing Josie to a doctor because she had gained a few pounds. What did we want? It was bad enough that a doctor was jabbing her finger, taking tubes and tubes of good blood from her, making her swallow liquid chalk. If it made us happy to throw our money away like that, all right. But here was this innocent dog, healthy and happy, and I was rushing her to a doctor. Then she summed it all up philosophically with, "Well, that's show business!"

Nevertheless we arrived at Dr. White's bright and early the following day. We saw Dr. Green. Dr. White was in surgery. Dr. Green actually gaped in amazement when he saw Josie. What were we doing? Pumping air into her? Once I assured him she was not pregnant he ordered instant X-rays. Something had to show up.

And it did. Acres and acres of fat! Nothing more. Dr. Green sent for Dr. Black. Dr. Black suggested an all-out consultation. Perhaps even keeping her overnight to await a special examination with *the* Dr. White. After all, maybe it was glandular.

I refused to leave Josie overnight. As it was she began shaking a block away from the establishment and never stopped until she was safely out of the door and down the street. I didn't want to subject her to any unnecessary anxiety.

They demanded to know exactly what I fed her. I explained she really didn't eat too much. The standard one meal a day—only she had it at two in the morning. It consisted of steak tidbits from Danny's

Hideaway, Toots Shor's, The Little Club, or Lindy's. At noon she shared my coffee, and maybe had a few biscuits and Yummies throughout the day. But nothing more.

A new regime was ordered immediately. Yummies were out! No more biscuits. No coffee. One meal a day—but not from Danny's Hideaway. The one meal was to consist of half a can of dog food. And that was it! We were to stick to this Spartan schedule for one month. If there were not an appreciable loss of weight, extensive tests would be in order. Because then it had to be glandular, maybe even thyroid.

I rushed home and threw out every biscuit and Yummy. Josie stared at me as if I had suddenly gone mad. In the mornings I took my coffee behind a closed door so as not to tempt her. At the end of two weeks I put her on the scale. She had gained a pound and a half!

I was hysterical. I didn't want to subject her to all those tests. Maybe exercise would help. Yes, that was it! All this lounging around and getting her belly rubbed was contributing to her obesity. It would make anyone's glands sluggish. Naturally I didn't tell any of these things to my mother-in-law. She'd only blame it on the doctor.

That night I set my alarm for nine in the morning. From now on Josie and I were going to take an hour's hike in the park. Maybe that would turn the tide.

I almost changed my mind about the whole thing when the alarm went off the following morning. But I knew it had to be done! My mother-in-law was an early riser—I could hear her puttering around in the kitchen. I crept out of bed quietly so as not to disturb Irving. There was no sign of Josie, but I figured she was still sleeping in her usual spot under my bed.

I decided to let her have an extra few minutes of sleep while I grabbed a cup of coffee. I headed for the kitchen to join my mother-in-law. I knew she'd be surprised to see me up at this hour.

As I stumbled drowsily across the living room, I suddenly became aware of all sorts of charming conversation emanating from the kitchen. My mother-in-law was doing the conversing. Josie was answering with exuberant squeals. The conversation went something like this:

"Now finish your oatmeal, Josie, and then I'll give you your soft-boiled eggs. No Josie, you can't have the eggs until all the oatmeal is finished. Here darling, I'll put some more sweet cream on it. Now, isn't that tasty?"

I held on to the door for strength. When I did speak, I croaked, "Good morning, girls."

My mother-in-law was delighted to see me. "How come you're up so early? Sit down. I think there's just enough oatmeal left." She scooped some into a plate for me.

"Mom." I made my voice gentle. "I thought you said you never fed Josie."

She looked at me in genuine surprise. "Would I let a dog die of starvation? I said I never fed her between meals. You're the one who does that, with those sawdust Yummies and coffee at noon."

Slowly I began to get the picture. "And what meals do you feed her?"

"Just the ordinary ones. The hours you and Irving keep aren't right for such a little animal. So I see to it that she has a good breakfast, lunch, and dinner. It's the least I can do for you while I stay here."

"What do you give her for lunch?" (It was torture, but I had to know.)

"Well that all depends," she explained. "Sometimes a little boiled chicken and peas and carrots. Sometimes fish. I make sure there's no bones. And sometimes we eat dairy. Sour cream and vegetables—or cheese blintzes. She adores my mushroom and barley soup, but I think soup is a little too gassy."

"And dinner?" I was fascinated with the life of this furry little Henry the Eighth.

"Well, you and Irving always insist that I don't cook dinner and have room service. But who can eat such big portions? So she shares it with me and it works out fine. Don't worry, I see to it that she has a well-rounded diet. Don't forget, I raised Irving and always saw to it that he ate plenty of fruit and vegetables. It was a long time ago, but I haven't forgotten."

She leaned down to pick up the empty egg plate, and I watched with fascinated horror as she poured a mixture of heavy cream, milk, coffee, and sugar into a plate.

"I add just a spoonful of coffee," she apologized. "It's the only way I can get her to drink her quart of milk a day. At lunch I add a little chocolate syrup. Irving hated milk when he was little too. But a quart of milk a day is a must for everyone. You and Irving should drink milk too." Then she said to Josie who was backing away from the half-finished plate, "Finish the milk sweetheart. Do it for Grandma." Grandma! Sweetheart, who knew where her next meal was coming from, obligingly returned to the dish and lapped up the remainder of Grandma's brew.

Grandma beamed and picked her up and cooed, "Good girl. Now kiss Grandma and go play a little." Josie bestowed a wet kiss on her personal chef, and Grandma who was puckered up like a suction pump, received it with maternal pride.

"When did the 'Grandma' bit begin?" I asked

Grandma smiled. "Well, when you get to know her, you realize that besides being cute, she's really a very nice person. And it pleases her to call me Grandma."

Of course I sat "Grandma" down and gave her the facts of life. I explained that no matter how human a dog was, it still had to follow a few canine rules. Like eating.

Grandma disagreed. You dress a dog up like a human being. You let it sleep in bed like a human being. You treat it like a human being. Then suddenly you want to feed it like a dog. Why? They had lungs, a liver, two kidneys, all the same inner equipment found in human beings.

I explained that a dog only needed one meal a day.

"One meal a day!" Grandma was horrified. "Who said so?"

I said the vet said so. Grandma sniffed. A lot he knew. That's why he was a vet instead of a real doctor.

Then Grandma came up with a gasser. It seems she had been doing some inquiring about dogs on her own with some very nice ladies she had met in the park. Did I know a dog had two stomachs?

I thought I had her there. "Yes. A dog does have two stomachs. Because they don't actually chew their food. They swallow it whole and use the other stomach to digest the food."

Grandma nodded in triumph. "We eat three meals a day with just one stomach to fill. Who's the professor who says a dog should eat just one meal a day when it has two stomachs to fill?"

Who could fight such logic? Besides, Grandma's tests were almost concluded and she was due to depart for Brooklyn at the end of the week, so I let her win the argument.

On the day of her departure I felt very sad as I watched Irving carry her bags to the car. Irving had to accompany her to Brooklyn alone because I didn't dare leave Josie. Grandma's departure had left her in a state of shock. But I was delighted to be able to call the vet and tell him to forget about the glandular business. Josie had no thyroid trouble. Josie had had an orgy!

19

Sex and the Single Dog

As SPRING slipped into summer, and the asphalt on the streets grew sticky and warm, Josephine made it clear that this was no season to take extended walks. Josephine wasn't against walking, but the climate had to be right. The winter was out because she hated snow. She also hated rain. From June until September it was too hot. The way I clocked it, there were about three days in October that came up with the necessary climatic requirements. And this certainly was not the right attitude for a dog with a weight problem.

But in July she met Moppet. Moppet was a cocoa-brown standard. She was two years older than Josie and six times Josie's size. But Moppet and Josie had a great deal in common. They both had show-business backgrounds.

Although Josephine still treated Bobo Eichenbaum like a dog, her snobbishness did not extend to all poodles. In fact, she really had nothing against poodles. Some of her best friends were poodles. She just didn't want to marry one. Therefore, she found it safer to restrict her friendship to the females of the breed, and among her poodle girlfriends, Josie was known to be quite gregarious and outgoing.

Especially with Moppet. Although Moppet wasn't a performer herself, she was in show business by osmosis. She belonged to Lee Reynolds, who at the time worked as Jackie Gleason's production assistant and general casting director. Jackie had a large combination office and apartment at the Park Sheraton Hotel. Lee and Moppet went to work there every day.

When Mr. Gleason hired Lee, he had no idea he was getting a package deal. Neither did Lee. But Lee soon found out that when Moppet was left alone in the apartment, Moppet sulked. And when this dog sulked, she didn't fool around. She was the furniture-chewing-type sulker. Of course Josie had done away with a few throw pillows in her day, but you must remember Moppet was a Standard. To her, a throw pillow was just an hors d'oeuvre. It was nothing for Moppet to devour an entire club chair or polish off the leg of the new coffee table for dessert.

Lee solved the problem by bringing Moppet to the office each day. Moppet adored the activity of show business and stopped eating furniture. She became intimate friends with the entire staff, and since she was a Gleason fan from way back, she literally worshiped the "Great One." He, in turn, thought she was quite a dog, so all around it was an extremely happy setup.

Lee took Moppet to the park on her lunch hour, and since Lee and I were friends, Josie struck up an immediate kinship with Moppet. As the weeks passed, Josie's friendship toward Moppet blossomed into open adoration. She followed Moppet around with the hero worship small children often display for an older girl.

When the show went off the air for the summer, Jackie Gleason went to his summer estate in Peekskill, New York. He had been gone less than a week when he called Lee and announced that he missed Moppet. He also announced that the country was the only place for a dog. How about if he sent his man down for Moppet?

Lee declined the generous offer. Especially after I

filled her in on Josephine's enthusiasm for the Concord and all its glorious mountain air. But Gleason insisted. Moppet should know the thrill of running free across acres and acres of grass. Why not let her have a fling at country living for just one week? He promised to take excellent care of her.

Once again Lee declined. Moppet was happy not being free. Moppet adored walking in Central Park on a leash. She had never run across acres and acres of grass. Maybe she wouldn't like it. Besides, as Lee explained, this was not exactly the time to let Moppet run loose. Because if Moppet did run loose and met up with a boy poodle, Moppet would become a mother. Gleason got the picture. But he insisted Lee had nothing to worry about. There wasn't a dog around for miles.

In the end a compromise was effected. Moppet would try it for a weekend. After all, Lee didn't want to deny Moppet a crack at glorious country living. Just because Josie was a confirmed city dweller—maybe Moppet was different. Nevertheless, she handed Moppet over with a brave smile that hid many misgivings.

Moppet extended her stay with Gleason for two action-packed weeks. According to Gleason, everything had come off just dandy. At first Moppet had just sat and stared at the acres and acres of grass. She didn't know what to do with them. But then, as Gleason put it, they had run into a windfall. Mrs. Orhbach, who lived nearby, suddenly arrived with a sweet motherly old collie. And this collie knew every inch of Peekskill. It immediately took Moppet under its wing and taught her the mysteries of country living —chasing rabbits, falling into streams, and digging up lawns for prehistoric roast-beef bones.

When Moppet returned, Josephine fell all over her, extending a warm welcome, she really had missed Moppet. But Moppet no longer showed the same enthusiasm for Central Park. She regarded it as a commercial structure. And Josie was a slob compared to the Orhbach collie. But as the days passed, she readjusted, and only an occasional longing look that she tossed to a passing squirrel told us she was recalling her thrilling sojourn at Peekskill.

Soon Moppet even went back to her old closeness with Josephine. And Moppet was a wonderful influence on Josie in the park. Being a large dog, she required real exercise. To Josie, the park was nothing more than a landscaped outhouse. Once she accomplished her mission, she was eager to cross the street and return home.

Because Moppet liked to exercise, Moppet had that wonderful concave upswing under her rib cage. And under Moppet's influence, Josie did manage an occasional scamper up and down a small hill.

Moppet had been home about three weeks when I suddenly noticed the absence of that wonderful concave look. I pointed it out to Lee. Was Moppet eating more than usual?

Lee said Moppet was not eating more than usual. Moppet just needed a haircut. Moppet had the haircut. But Moppet did not have any concave look. Moppet had put on weight. Lee began extending the walks. Lee lost six pounds, but Moppet continued to thrive. Finally, Lee voiced the horrible thought that was rumbling in both our minds.

Had it *really* been a lady collie?

She phoned Gleason who was still in Peekskill. Gleason was positive it was a lady collie.

Lee relaxed. "You mean Mrs. Orhbach told you it was a girl?"

"Who needs to be told such a thing?" Gleason roared. "When I saw it, I just knew!"

Lee suddenly didn't feel quite as relaxed. "How did you know, Jackie, dear?"

"Because I know a dame when I see one! And this

was a dame. It had long hair and . . . well . . . it just looked like a broad. That's all!"

Lee rushed Moppet to the doctor. The results proved Gleason might be an excellent judge of pulchritude of the human species, but when it came to collies, he was a complete zero. Moppet was definitely in the "family way."

Lee was near collapse. A collie and a poodle! What would emerge? A copoodle! What would she do with them? They'd be monsters! She wouldn't be able to *give* them away. And yet she was responsible for them. After all, they were Moppet's flesh and fur.

She called Mr. Gleason. Mr. Gleason called Mrs. Orhbach. Then Mr. Gleason called Miss Reynolds. A very abashed Mr. Gleason. After abject apologies, he tried to point out the good features of the situation. After all, it wasn't as if Moppet had just gotten mixed up with some unknown dog. This was a very good collie. It came from an excellent family—all of its ancestors were show dogs. Maybe the whole thing would work out fine. After all, mixed marriages were often extremely successful.

Naturally, everyone offered Lee suggestions. Great quantities of Castor Oil often did the trick. And what about those shots? Then there was always Denmark— or was it Sweden? But Lee felt it was safest to let nature take its course.

Moppet would go through the ordeal and give birth to heaven-knows-what, but Mr. Gleason would personally have to guarantee that each monstrosity was adopted and given a good and loving home. Naturally, the embarrassed Mr. Gleason meekly swore to this agreement.

In due course, the copoodles were born. Now collies are beautiful. And poodles are beautiful. But as a blend, it was a mess! They were a muddy red brown, with white spots, and boasted poodle faces, collie ears, and long collie legs. Even Moppet couldn't quite believe her eyes. She loved them, but she never failed to do a "take" at the sight of them. Of course, like any mother, she probably felt they would outgrow this strange, ungainly look.

Each day Lee phoned Gleason and said, "Well?"

And Gleason would reply, "I'm giving the matter serious thought."

When they were three months of age, Lee was still stuck with them and Gleason was still thinking about them. So one day Lee bundled them up and brought them to Mr. Gleason's office.

He stared. "Holy smokes, they are ugly! What are we going to do with them?"

Lee smiled sweetly. "We are going to do nothing. You are going to get them good foster homes."

"But who figured they'd look like this? What do I say to people?"

"Say they have wonderful personalities, once you get to know them."

"Take them home for another few months," Gleason pleaded. "Maybe they'll straighten out."

"The bigger they get, the uglier they'll be," Lee argued. "You know what they all say. All puppies are cute. And believe it or not, these are puppies!"

Well, never let it be said that Jackie Gleason is not a man of his word. That night he and his chauffeur bundled up the puppies and drove upstate. They stopped at the first house they saw and rang the bell. When the door opened, there stood Gleason with a dejected look, holding a copoodle.

"Madam," he said softly, "a poodle who is a personal friend of mine had a wild weekend with a collie. Then, cad that he is, he deserted her. Would you take one of her children? I can't mention the name of this cad, but he does come from a very fine family."

And that's how it went. He stopped at every house along the way. Now, if you lived in the country and Jackie Gleason rang your doorbell and personally guaranteed such a piece of merchandise, would you reject it? Why, those copoodles were grabbed up with frantic delight. Like a collector's item. They became the celebrities of the neighborhood. After all, anyone can have a poodle. Anyone can have a collie. But who can have a copoodle given to him personally by Jackie Gleason?

Just seven lucky people in the Catskill Mountains!

20

Cousin Tony for a While

Once Moppet's puppies had been placed, she reappeared in Central Park, her old carefree, frisky self. Her figure returned and by midwinter she had forgotten the collie, Peekskill, and even the seven strange children she had whelped. She looked forward to her daily meetings with Josie. But Josephine's enchantment with Moppet came to an abrupt halt. It was nothing personal. It was strictly climatic. Josephine had now celebrated her third birthday and she was very "hip." She knew there was such a thing as seasons. And to her, winter in Central Park was for the pigeons! Yet Moppet acted as if it was just as much fun to frisk about on a ten-degree day as any other day. She kept beckoning Josie to follow her up and down a hill for a bit of a prance. Josephine, the hothouse flower, merely stood there in her little red coat and shivered miserably. She'd stare at Moppet and then tug the leash in the direction of home.

Soon she even took to avoiding Moppet. If she saw Moppet leaping down a hill, Josie would pretend to be nearsighted, and quickly drag me in another direction.

I was sorry to see her lose Moppet as a friend, but with Josie, fate always seemed to intervene, and something would come up. It did—on a bright clear day in February.

My phone rang at eight in the morning. It was

Joyce Mathews Rose. "I have a new dog!" she shouted.

In the gray darkness of the dawn, I groped for a cigarette and tried to sound enthusiastic. "Wonderful. But how does Toulouse feel about it?"

"Oh I haven't got Toulouse anymore."

I was suddenly wide awake. I hated the thoughts that came to my mind. Because Toulouse is not the kind of dog you can give away.

But she reassured me. "Billy just couldn't stand Toulouse another day. So when my mother told me she knew a family in Huntington, Long Island that was just dying for a dog, I packed him right off."

"They might send him right back," I suggested.

"No," she said cheerfully. "They weren't looking for a stunning French poodle. They just wanted a dog. And Toulouse does look like a dog. We have to admit that. I've talked to them; they think he's wonderful. Toulouse will be very happy. And now I have an adorable dachshund."

"Good luck." I was all for terminating the conversation and going back to sleep. Irving was beginning to stir, and besides, dachshunds never particularly thrilled me.

But Joyce wanted to chat. "This is a real prize."

"Joyce, remember all babies are adorable."

Irving sat up. "Who had a baby?"

"Joyce. A dachshund."

Irving yawned. "What time is it?"

"Ten after eight."

Irving yawned. "In the *morning?*"

I didn't like the tone of his voice. "Joyce, I'll talk to you later."

"Don't hang up or I'll only call back," Joyce threatened.

Josephine came to life and rumbled out from under the bed. She leaped up and industriously began to give

Irving his early morning kisses. She was punch drunk at the hour, but figured she had overslept.

"Go to sleep, Josie," Irving groaned. "It's still night-time."

"Joyce," I whispered, "I've got to hang up. Irving and Josie are still asleep."

"We've been up for hours," Joyce said happily. "Even Billy has had breakfast."

"Well let the dachshund get some sleep. Babies need rest."

"Oh it's not a baby. It's two years old. This time Billy wasn't taking any chances. Its name is Tony and it has a pedigree a mile long. It's had all its shots, it's healthy—nothing can happen to this one."

"I hope you'll both be very happy together." I started to replace the receiver.

"We'll be over in an hour."

"And we'll be asleep!"

"Come on," Joyce pleaded. "Didn't I help you give Josie Pepto-Bismol?"

"But Tony isn't sick."

"No, but he wants to meet Josie."

"Can't he wait till the afternoon?"

"We'll be over in an hour." Joyce hung up before I could shout another objection. It was just as well. Irving was awake and Josie was bringing her third squeak toy to the bed.

I must admit it was a great meeting. It was love at first sight on Tony's part. He had never seen a poodle before and he stood there gaping with admiration and worship.

Josie's contact with dachshunds had been limited to an amazed stare the few times she had passed one in the park. She knew we were all God's creatures and that some of us were not born perfect, so her heart went out to Tony. She had seen a lot of dogs, and the way she figured it, no dog was supposed to look like that.

Tony knew he did not look like Josephine. But he knew he was a dog. A license-carrying member of the same race. Tony had been raised on a fancy breeding farm with other dachshunds. He was well-informed about the mysteries of sex. Although still a pure young bachelor, he too was "hip." After all, Tony had lived with the trees. He had also lived intimately with rain. He had seen birds do it, squirrels do it, he had even seen the bees do it—so like Cole Porter says, "Let's fall in love."

Naturally he knew a bee loved a bee and a squirrel loved a squirrel. But he loved Josephine! Of course he realized he couldn't propose to her in his present state. But he wasn't worried. Remember, Tony had lived with nature. He knew nature took its course. Things changed. He had seen caterpillars turn into butterflies and then go off with other butterflies. So he gazed at Josie with adoration, and decided to wait. He'd wait for the day when he would wake up and find himself a poodle.

He never doubted that this miracle would take place. And happy with the thought of this blissful future, he was content with the wonderful present. He watched Josie and took on all her virtues. He rejected his little wicker bed and slept with Joyce. He developed a tremendous appetite. Only Tony really had something going for him. First he'd share Joyce's breakfast tray. Then he'd trundle into Billy's room and beg a few tidbits from him. Then there was the butler's pantry to visit. Billy and Joyce were always watching their weight, so Tony had his real breakfast with the cook and butler. Like pancakes and sausage. Tony really had a wonderful life. Tony got love and affection from everyone. Tony also got very fat.

Since Josie was due for her spring checkup, Joyce decided to bring Tony along. Dr. White's staff was dumbstruck when they saw him. In fact they ignored Josie's ever-increasing great white belly—Josie weighed in at seventeen pounds. Dr. Black merely made the notation with a shrug of despair. (Naturally we didn't see Dr. White. He was in surgery.)

But Dr. Black's eyes actually bulged at Tony's measurements. He placed him on the floor and watched him walk. Tony didn't walk, he waddled! You couldn't even see his legs. Dr. Black began to give Joyce the facts of life on dachshunds. They carried a long body and spine on four short legs. A heavy dachshund was a cinch to dislocate a disc. And a sudden leap could even snap a bone and paralyze the dog.

We each paid our five dollars and made a hurried exit. From there we journeyed to my apartment where we discussed the situation over a Scotch while Josie and Tony busied themselves munching away at some Yummies.

"Look how happy they are," Joyce beamed. "Personally, I think it's just a theory and not a fact," she continued as she tossed Tony a salted peanut. "Today we think slim people are the healthy ones. A generation ago you had to be plump to be healthy. Who knows, ten years from now the cycle might reverse itself."

I asked what she was getting at?

"Why should Tony and Josie starve because the vets are going through a 'keep-them-thin' cycle?" She tossed Tony another peanut. Josie stared at me and moaned in envy.

I held out. "But insurance companies say thin people live longer than fat people. Not just vets. People doctors also agree with this theory. Look at the big holler about cholesterol and animal fat."

"I've met an awful lot of fat doctors and fat insurance men," Joyce offered.

I had to admit she had a point. Look at Edith Piaf. She weighed only ninety pounds and spent most of her adult life going in and out of hospitals. Yet Sophie Tucker, who is no ad for Metrecal, is still going strong. I began to waver. Josie must have read my mind because she drooled and moaned.

I hesitated for three more seconds, then poured another drink for Joyce, another for myself, placed the whole dish of peanuts on the floor for the ecstatic dogs, and said, "Here's to a gay and gastric life!"

And that's how it went. I tossed out the canned dog food and Josie returned to the thrilling steak tidbits from Danny's Hideaway. Yummies and Lollypups flowed by the handful. Josie spent the next six months in epicurian delight. Tony became known as Ninety-third Street's answer to King Farouk! Six months later, on Josie's fourth birthday, she tipped the scales at eighteen pounds. And the following day, Tony dropped dead!

The autopsy claimed he died of a brain hemorrhage, but his spine was in marvelous condition. Good enough to be put on display at the Smithsonian Institution. So Joyce had that consolation. Because everyone knows brain hemorrhages have nothing to do with calories. At least Tony had known the delights of braised duck, soufflés, and smoked salmon.

Nevertheless, Tony's sudden demise left me a little shaken. I threw out the Yummies and went back to the canned dog food. Instead of citing Winston Churchill, I began to spout about George Bernard Shaw. He ate only grass and lived till he was almost a hundred!

Joyce was inconsolable. So Billy, who is great in all emergencies, rushed out and surprised her with a brand-new fawn-colored girl dachshund. It was named Baby Doll. Within a week Baby Doll had filled the gap in Joyce's heart. Of course no one would ever replace Tony, but in her special way she loved Baby Doll just as intensely.

I liked Baby Doll too. It was Josephine who concerned us. How were we going to break it to her. She was so young and innocent. She knew nothing about death. She might even go into shock over Tony. After all, he had been her best buddy-buddy.

Irving came up with a wild suggestion. It was so wild I figured it might just work. Since Josie knew very little about dachshunds, it might never occur to her that God created an entire breed of such apparitions. To her, Tony was just one of nature's mistakes. It might be possible to pass Baby Doll off as Tony.

We arranged the great meeting at my apartment. Baby Doll whisked in and greeted Josie with the enthusiasm of a lifelong buddy. (Thank God for her youth and outgoing personality.) There was a tense moment when Josie just stood and stared.

Joyce and I cooed, "It's your little friend Tony—only now we call him . . . her . . . Baby Doll. It's like a pet name, Josie"

Josie continued to stare. Finally she gingerly approached Baby Doll. She did an awful lot of extra sniffing and even seemed a little surprised at some of her findings. But as I have said before, Josie is a very adjusted dog, so she took it all in her stride. She accepted Baby Doll as if every day a black dachshund turned beige. And if some of Tony's usual equipment was missing, well that's the way the Yummy crumbles. It was his problem, not hers!

21

This Is Friendship!

Josephine saw a great deal of Baby Doll throughout the spring. Joyce tried to keep Baby Doll on a diet, and I remained fairly strict with Josie. Of course she cheated a few times. After all, when one is invited to someone's home for dinner, one cannot refuse the hostess' succulent dishes and demand a half a can of dog food. At least Josie couldn't. And Josie was invited to dinner quite often. Especially by Last-One Hershkowitz. Before I go into any explanations, I guess I'd better explain Last-One's name.

Last-One comes from a large family. Her mother either had a divine disposition or a great sense of humor or both, because she permitted her husband to name all the children. The first-born was a girl. She was named Lebanon. (They were living in Lebanon then.) A brother arrived. He was called Harlem. (They had moved.) The next child was a girl and was called Portland. (They moved a lot.) Portland later married Fred Allen and went on to radio fame as Portland Hoffa. James Mason named his daughter after Portland. Being an Englishman, maybe he thought this was an everyday American name. Anyway he liked the sound of it. So you can see that this eccentricity of Mr. Hoffa's will probably perpetuate throughout many new generations.

Content with his little family of Lebanon, Harlem, and Portland, Mr. Hoffa decided to call it quits in the propagation department. But Mrs. Hoffa had a mind of her own and brought forth another infant girl. Mr. Hoffa put his foot down and dramatically named this final baby Last-One.

But don't underestimate the late Mrs. Hoffa's independence of spirit. Mr. Hoffa might name them, but she produced them. Another bouncing baby girl arrived on the scene. This time Mrs. Hoffa figured she might get lucky and wind up with a "Janie" or "Mary." After all, how could Mr. Hoffa top a name like Last-One. He did. He named the new baby Period.

Mrs. Hoffa knew when she was licked. She stopped producing babies. Maybe she was afraid another baby might be called "Exclamation Mark" or "You're Kidding." So she conceded and Period was the last of her issue.

Oddly enough, as they grew up, none of the children seemed to mind the unusual names. As Last-One put it, it proved an asset. People rarely forgot her name. Of course every time she was introduced to someone new, she invariably got the same reaction. A wide stare, followed with, "What did you say your name was?" And then a disbelieving, "Yes, that's what I thought you said."

So no one ever forgot her name. And if someone was walking down the street and they said, "Oh I ran into Last-One today," no one ever said, "Last-One who?"

Last-One acquired the Hershkowitz when she married an attorney named Arthur Hershkowitz. Last-One and Artie live nearby, and we often spend an evening together relaxing in the cultural pursuits of gin rummy and TV. Last-One is a sensational cook. Very often she would call on the spur of the moment and say, "If you haven't anything planned, come on over. I've got a big roast beef. And be sure to bring Josephine." (You will please note that the "Bring Josephine" is a direct quote from Last-One, not a suggestion of mine.)

Last-One was anything but a dog lover. But Josie had completely captivated her. As a matter of fact, no one in her family was wild about dogs. Portland actively disliked them. She ran for the hills if one ever came within sniffing distance.

Josie loved to spend an evening at the Hershkowitz' She even recognized the building when she was a block away and would begin to strain at the leash to get there. Very often when I wasn't even going to Last-One's but had to pass her building, Josie would pull a sit-down strike and refuse to budge. And whether I chose to or not, we had to pay a little social call on Last-One.

There were many things about Last-One that appealed to Josie. First and foremost, there was Last-One's kitchen. Josephine had never seen a real kitchen before. And a kitchen the size of a living room, bursting with exotic aromas was enough to attract even the most blasé poodle—let alone a girlish type like Josie, who lived to eat! So it was only natural that she looked upon Last-One as someone very special.

It wasn't enough that when we sat down to eat, Josie was served a special plate of roast beef or turkey with all the trimmings. Last-One also came up with extracurricular little surprises for her. Since we always had a drink before dinner, Last-One didn't want Josie to just sit around twiddling her paws in boredom, so she'd say, "Look, Josie, look what Aunt Last-One has for you. Hors d'oeuvres!" And she'd place three or four beautiful crisp warm chicken livers before the cherished guest. Now chicken liver is Josephine's favorite dish, and it's also a rare treat since I am not exactly a Prudence Penny in the kitchen.

And there were other things about Last-One besides the kitchen and the chicken livers that enthralled Josephine. Take the three-tiered candy dish in the living room. Josie had seen candy dishes before, but this one was like the Eiffel Tower come to life. One tier contained chocolate buds, another gum drops, and another hard candy.

Then there was the coffee table that was always stacked with little goodies like pretzels, walnuts and on rare occasions, jelly beans. I think Last-One created this do-it-yourself Schraffts when she gave up smoking.

Since a visit to Last-One's was such a festive event I was deeply appreciative of her thoughtfulness in including Josie in all our invitations. I immediately put Last-One high on my "friends-for-life" list.

One night when we were sitting around playing gin rummy after a particularly sumptuous dinner, Portland (who lives in the same building) dropped down unexpectedly for a social call. Josephine was prone on the floor, taking a short respite to build up sufficient energy to attack the three-tiered candy dish. Among Josie's multiple talents is the ability to keep one eye open while she is in a state of heavy slumber. This is important just in case anything unexpected comes up —like Portland. Naturally Josephine forced herself into action the moment Portland arrived. Last-One shot me a quick "Porty-is-afraid-of-dogs" look.

Portland entered, greeted us all, and then came up with the amazing observation. "Oh, there's a dog here."

We all agreed that it was indeed a dog and Irving and I took bows on the ownership along with oaths that it did not bite and wouldn't even come near her.

With this assurance, Portland settled on the couch contentedly. "Now you all go on with your gin game. I've brought my knitting. You're positive that hoont won't come near me, aren't you?"

"Of course not, Portland," I assured her. "She doesn't take to strangers."

Last-One started to open her mouth in protest, but I kicked her and said, "Deal the cards."

Portland said, "Then how come she's suddenly sitting on the couch beside me?"

I said that was very unusual. And very flattering because as a rule Josephine was very reserved. Everyone was silent as the cards were dealt. Last-One and Artie tried to look nonchalant.

Portland spoke again. "Why in hell is she jabbing at my arm with her paw?"

I kept my voice casual and played my hand. "That means she wants you to rub her belly." Last-One looked like she was going to faint.

Portland started at Josie. "I've never rubbed a dog's belly." I told her to give it a whirl. Irving knocked with ten points. I went gin on Last-One.

Suddenly Portland said, "When I stop rubbing her belly, she gives me a jab with the paw again. How about that? She's smart all right."

I suggested she rub her belly some more.

"I am," Portland answered, "But it's hard to knit with just one hand. Say, how about this!" Portland continued. "If I don't rub the right spot, she pushes my hand to where she wants to be rubbed!"

We kept dealing the cards, waiting for the terrible moment when Portland would snap back to reality and remember she was afraid of dogs. For five minutes nothing was heard but the rustle of cards.

Then Portland spoke again. "Hey, this is the cutest hoont I've ever seen. You know, I don't like dogs, but this one is different. "

Everyone began to relax. Last-One caught me with forty points. Artie went gin on Irving. Portland put down her knitting and concentrated on full-time belly rubbing. "Listen, Jackie, I know you and Irving often go to the Coast on short trips. If you have to leave this hoont behind, I'll be glad to take her. She'd be great company. I've never known a dog like this."

Last-One was indignant. "Listen Portland, *this* is Josephine's home away from home. I'd be insulted if

Jackie ever left her with anyone but me. After all, she likes my cooking, Frances adores her, Artie is crazy about her."

Whereupon Mr. Hershkowitz said, "What Last-One says is true. This is a most unusual dog. I like her very much. She's an extremely nice dog too. In fact I'd welcome the idea of having her here. When Frances is away at school or camp, it gets very lonesome here."

Naturally this called for an answer from Mrs. Hershkowitz. And she came up with one. "What do you mean lonesome? What am I? A Waring Blender?"

Mr. Hershkowitz immediately came up with the proper and affectionate explanation. Last-One was indeed excellent company. But when Frances was away, he missed having a child in the house. Josie was just like a child.

Last-One agreed on that score. She also stated that she'd like Josephine's company as there were many evenings that *certain people* fell asleep in front of the television set. In fact, she insisted that the next time we went to the Coast, Josephine was to be her guest.

Of course I came up with the proper words of gratitude, but pointed out that Josie was accustomed to staying with Mr. Ingram and since raising dogs was his business, she might be better off with him.

Naturally I got, "You don't trust me with Josephine? After I raised Frances? Anyone who can raise a child can take care of a dog."

Well if you fight a statement like that you are put down as some kind of eccentric. Even though you know anyone who's raised a child does not necessarily know how to raise a dog! Or the other way around.

However two months later, rather than offend Last-One, I took the risk and deposited Josie at the Hershkowitz' for eight days. I packed a small bag for Josephine, put in her leash, her Yummies, her ball, a few other personal belongings, and my phone number at the Beverly Hills Hotel. Also the phone number of the vet.

I kissed her good-bye and told her to be a good girl (Josie, not Last-One). I walked to the door, knowing she would follow me. I braced myself to face the dreadful farewell scene. But it never came off. As I turned to wave bye-bye, Josie didn't even see me. She was too busy helping herself to five or six chocolate buds!

22

This Is Friendship?

In spite of everything, I worried while I was on the Coast. Just because Last-One could knock off a great roast beef didn't mean she knew a dry warm nose meant fever. Had I warned her about chicken bones? Children can eat chicken and know about leaving the bones. But a chicken bone can kill a dog. Yet a roast-beef bone is permissible. And the Pepto-Bismol—I had forgotten to tell her about that! When we returned we dashed right from the airport to Last-One's to retrieve our angel.

Artie, Last-One, and Josie were all waiting for us. But they looked tired. Everyone looked tired. Like maybe they had been on a bender. Even Josie had circles under her eyes. Irving asked what was up?

Last-One said, "Josephine. All night. Every night." Then she added, "I have a few little questions I'd like you to clear up for me. What in hell kind of sleeping hours does this dog keep?"

"My hours," I answered.

Last-One sighed. "*Now* you tell me."

It seems that she had expected to rear Josie like a small child. Or at least like a dog. Accordingly, she had risen at seven, her usual hour, and before giving Artie his breakfast, planned to rush Josie outside to the curb. After all, it is a known fact that dogs wake in the morning brimming with energy and pep, raring to go! When you show them the leash they dance with joy at the prospect of a short brisk hike in the fresh morning air. But not Josephine.

First of all, at seven, when everyone leaped out of bed, there was no sign of Josephine. Everyone called her name and shouted, but she failed to make an appearance. After a careful search, she was discovered curled up in a little ball under the bed, sound asleep.

Last-One crawled under and made happy little clucking noises. "Wake up, honey, it's morning time!" Josephine yawned and inched deeper into snug comfort under the bed.

Last-One stretched out her arm and cooed, "Come on out, Josie. Aunt Lasty is calling you."

Josie inched farther away from her reach. Soon it developed into an all-out tug of war. Last-One finally latched onto one of Josie's legs and dragged Josie into the living room. Unfortunately she released Josie as she went in search of her leash. In a flash Josie dived back under the bed to grab another forty winks.

After another skirmish under the bed, Josie was dragged out into the street and plunked before a curb. Bleary-eyed, but being the good-natured angel that she is, Josie performed in the manner expected. This was done more as a gesture to please Last-One than to relieve her own kidneys. Then she turned and dragged Last-One back to the apartment.

Last-One turned her attention toward getting Artie and Frances their breakfasts. Then letting bygones be bygones, she sang out gaily, "Josie, here's your biscuit. Your breakfast, honey."

But was there the patter of little feet? No. Sleeping Beauty had returned to her haven under the bed and was snoring away.

Like most women, Last-One has her set routine about the house. Once Artie and Frances have departed, she attends to her chores. By noon the beds are made and everything is spotless. Then, a cat nap on the living room couch. By one o'clock she is refreshed and ready to spend her afternoon on the outside.

But at noon, just as Last-One was lying down to rest, Josie emerged, her old sparkling self. *Now* she wanted breakfast. Well, Last-One decided she was going to straighten this dog out. Teach her about respectable hours and clean wholesome living. She started with the long walks. At least three or four during the day. And after dinner each night, she dragged Josie on a ten-block hike. After all, *every* dog likes to walk! Last-One said if she hadn't known better she would have almost believed that Josie kept pulling her over to hail a cab.

But the nights were the worst. Last-One and Artie retired early. Like ten o'clock. At ten o'clock Josie's personality was in full bloom. She was at the peak of activity—ready for endless hours of ball playing and belly rubbing. At home she never missed Jack Paar and the "Late Late Show." But at ten o'clock, at the Hershkowitz', everyone went to bed. Except Josephine.

When they put out the lights she dashed from their room to their daughter's room with a wild look that shouted, "What's up? Has everyone suddenly gone crazy around here? It's the shank of the evening." Everyone tried to sleep. Except Josephine.

She began to pace. Now Last-One has nice shiny Venetian-type tile in her foyer. Unfortunately it amplified the patter of Josie's little feet as she frantically paced back and forth. Hour after hour she paced. Up and down. Artie and Last-One lay awake in the dark listening.

Last-One sighed at the end of her recital. "There wasn't a night that Josie hit the sack before 3 A.M."

I apologized to Last-One. It must have been rough on her. But at the same time it must have been equally rough on Josie. Josie is a "night person." It's a proven medical fact that some people function at their highest level in the late hours of the evening.

Last-One said just because I was that kind of a kook, there was no reason to inflict this kookiness on Josie. Children always ape people they adore. When Josie sees me sitting up till all hours, it's only natural for her to do the same. Like eating in bed. Then Last-One demanded to know where I ate my breakfast.

Now where does anyone have her morning coffee? In bed of course.

Then, prying even further into my private life, she asked, "And when you have this coffee, where does Josie have her dog biscuit?"

What a question! I live in a four-room hotel suite. What am I supposed to do? Be formal and send her out into the drawing room to eat it?

Well, it seems that in Last-One's house *everyone* sits at a table in the dining area when they have their breakfast—or any other form of nourishment. When Josephine finally did come to life at noon, Last-One handed her the dog biscuit. To her horror, Josie took the biscuit and leaped on Last-One's freshly made bed with the white organdy spread and began to munch away.

Well, how was Josie supposed to know? Our hotel maid never makes the bed until three in the afternoon. And we don't have white organdy spreads. We have white moire spreads and Josie is free to leap upon them whenever she feels so inclined. She has been leaping on these spreads since she was a baby and they are still in excellent condition. (Personally, I felt that if Last-One wanted to go fool around with organdy spreads, she deserved what she got!) But I kept these opinions to myself and merely asked Last-One how she had licked the problem.

Well, she hadn't exactly licked it, but she and Josie had worked out an effective compromise. Last-One didn't put on the organdy spreads until after Josie ate her biscuit. I apologized for the inconvenience and promised that Josie would spend her future vacations with Mr. Ingram.

To my surprise, Last-One got very indignant. "I want her to stay with me. For her own good. I didn't want to push any rules down her throat because this was our first time together. But she's a very bright dog and she'll fall into our way of living very quickly. She's living a very dissipated life with you. Maybe it's okay for you. You're an actress and statistics prove most actresses are a little crazy. They have to be to live through all the disappointments and setbacks and still keep at it."

"Last-One," I interrupted. "Are we gathered together to discuss the perils of my profession or Josephine's sleeping habits?"

"It's your profession that's ruining her. It's just not right for a poodle to go around acting like an actress. Josie is a very normal, bright, adjusted dog. If I had her for a month, I'd straighten her out."

I ignored the startled look in Josephine's eyes and politely agreed that she was welcome to Josie's companionship any time we went away. I wasn't worried. Of the two, Josie was by far the stronger personality, and I'd put her up against Last-One any time. If they remained together long enough, Josie was bound to emerge victorious. Strangely enough Artie came up with a few opinions that hinted he went along with my thinking.

"Last-One's not going to change her. My money's on Josephine all the way. This dog has a mind of her own. She's already got each of us categorized on her own private "sucker" list. Last-One is the "cooking sucker." Frances is the "ball-throwing sucker." And I'm the "belly-rubbing sucker.""

Naturally Josie sent Last-One a gorgeous white bag as a happy-happy for her stay. She sent Frances some perfume and Artie a bottle of his favorite Scotch. At least they could never say Josie didn't know all the social graces.

Last-One adored the gifts but insisted Josephine shouldn't have bothered. It had been a pleasure having her. And once again she reminded me that whenever we had to travel she would expect Josie as a house guest.

However, six months later, when we found it necessary to go to the Coast again, Irving said we ought to give the Last-One–Josephine situation some careful thought. Of course it was nice for Josie to spend a week with close friends like Last-One and Artie, rather than be an impersonal paying guest at Mr. Ingram's. But as a paying guest she was catered to. Mr. Ingram didn't go around trying to remodel her living habits. If she wanted breakfast in bed, fine! That's what we were paying for. Personalized service. If she wanted to stay up and watch the "Late Show," that was all right too. And when he returned her, he always said, "She was delightful. What a personality. No trouble at all." We didn't have to listen to a sermon about how our girl was going to the dogs, living a decadent life, ruining his sleep.

So I told Last-One that maybe Josie would be better off at Mr. Ingram's as I didn't want to cause them any trouble and Josie was still keeping her show business hours.

Last-One got very upset. So did Artie. Didn't we trust Josephine in their care? So what if they had a few sleepless nights. Josephine would eventually fall into their routine.

Unless we wanted to dissolve a lifelong friendship, we had no alternative but to send her to the loving Hershkowitz'. Josephine was very tuned in to the whole situation. Although she adored Last-One, I think she was secretly rooting for a sojourn with Mr. Ingram; I noticed she did not bound into Last-One's apartment with her usual enthusiasm. I think she regarded it like a trip to a milk farm, or a required hitch of army basic training.

Ten days later when I went to retrieve Josephine, Last-One triumphantly announced she had licked the midnight to dawn pacing by allowing Josie to sleep in the same bed with her.

"You mean you didn't let her do that last time?" I

demanded. "Don't tell me she tried and you put her out of bed!"

Last-One stared. "You never told me that went with the deal. Whoever took in a house guest that expected to snuggle with you?"

No wonder poor Josie had paced. She had no security. She doesn't mind sleeping under a bed. In fact she prefers it. Just as long as she knows it's her bed, and that any given time during the night, she can leap on it and snuggle with the occupant. No one wants to sleep on the floor all night long.

Last-One said no one was forcing her to sleep on the floor. There were plenty of places besides under the covers with her. What was wrong with the couch in the living room? Or the club chairs? Josie slept beautifully on them during the day.

But Last-One had given in and let her snuggle. Anything was better than pacing. But as Last-One put it, if she had to snuggle, why couldn't she snuggle with Artie? Or Frances? Why did it have to be her? I asked her what she had against snuggling. Last-One didn't like to snuggle. When she went to sleep, she wanted to sleep. She didn't want to snuggle.

I refrained from offering any comments. After all, she and Artie had a very successful marriage and who was I to tell her how much fun she was missing? So I took Josie home and thanked her for the "use of her snuggling."

This time Josephine sent Last-One an Italian gold wrist watch. A few months later Josie went back to snuggle with Last-One again, and sent Last-One gold earrings to match the watch.

In the summer when we had to go to the Coast again, I deposited Josie with the bejeweled Last-One with an easy conscience. She still needed an Italian gold pin to round out the set. The following year, if things went well, I could start her on a pearl set.

When I returned, Last-One accepted the pin and

said, "You really shouldn't give me such lovely gifts
It isn't necessary." She put on the pin and admired i
in the mirror as she continued, "Besides, this is the las
time that slob of a dog is staying in this apartment."

Of course I started for her throat, but Irving re-
strained me. Using heroic calm, he demanded to know
what she had done this time.

Still admiring the pin, Last-One casually asked
"When was the last time that dog had a bath?"

Well! I grabbed Josie. We didn't have to take in-
sults like this! Josie was bathed and clipped every few
weeks and smelled like a geranium.

Last-One said that unfortunately it was summer, and
a very hot summer. And Josephine was getting more
and more devoted to her. Not only did she snuggle all
night in Last-One's arms, but she insisted on sitting in
her lap all day. And with the August humidity, Josephine was beginning to smell kind of gamy.

Irving calmed me down by reminding me how
shouting always upset Josephine. After all, Josie didn't
know I was threatening to kill Last-One. She thought
maybe I was hollering at her. I snuggled Josie and told
her we were only play acting. Then I shot a murderous glare at Last-One.

Last-One calmly sat down on the couch, polished
her new pin, and stated, "Jackie can shout all she
wants. It doesn't bother me. A fact is a fact. That dog
stinks."

Josephine, completely unaware that the rumpus concerned her personal hygiene, leaped on the couch and
began to cover Last-One's face with adoring kisses.

"Which reminds me," Last-One continued calmly,
"this dog could also use some Sen-Sen."

Well, that did it! I grabbed Josephine and said that
maybe Last-One didn't exactly smell like Chanel to
Josie, but that Josie was too polite to allow a little
thing like that to interfere with her affection for
someone.

Even Irving insisted that Josephine smelled just like a rose, and I told Last-One that it just proves you never really know a person until you live with her.

Last-One ignored this barb and calmly announced that she hoped this wouldn't hurt our friendship—that she still regarded Josie as a friend. It was just that she didn't want so much togetherness.

Artie said that Josie smelled just fine to him, but then he did have rose fever and couldn't smell anything—and Last-One always was extremely sensitive to smells. As a matter of fact, he said Last-One probably had the most over-developed smeller he had ever met.

Naturally Last-One turned and said a few things to Artie about how she had just the normal sense of smelling, and if he happened to have none, why make her out to be the neurotic one. He said she *was* a little neurotic about smells. Take his cigars for instance. She said his cigars smelled lousy!

And with the pleasant sounds of this little domestic chit-chat ringing in our ears, we grabbed Josie and silently stole into the night.

Of course I still see Last-One. I'm not the type to hold a grudge. We go out together, play cards together. I've forgotten all about it. It's only when my eyes fasten to the Italian gold wristwatch that graces her arm as she deals the cards, that I secretly toy with the idea of stabbing her!

23

Life Begins at Forty?

I REMEMBER reading somewhere of an aged lady who lay on her deathbed, and in a moment of sudden lucidity cried to herself, "I'm ninety-three and I'm dying! But how can that be, when I still feel in my heart that I'm eighteen?"

Strangely enough I can identify with her emotions. I've always felt eighteen. Even when I was five years old. And if I reach the formidable age of ninety-three I'll probably feel exactly like that little old lady. I don't think I'll be sitting around in lady-like purple or posing for portraits like Whistler's Mother. Of course this is all useless conjuring. I'll never make ninety. I figure somewhere in my eighties I'll either melt to death from nourishing creams, or strangle to death in a chin strap. In short, I have no intentions of aging gracefully. I will go out kicking, screaming, and fighting the battle of eternal youth!

Naturally Josephine feels the same way. Poodles are supposed to settle down after the age of two and give up ball playing and chew-toys. They are supposed to spend the rest of their lives sleeping and being ornamental. Yet at six years of age Josephine was still a Yogi Berra in the ball-playing department, and walked with the gait and trot of a puppy. To me she was a puppy, and she would have remained a puppy, if I wasn't the type who listened to every big-mouthed stranger I met in Central Park.

This particular Big Mouth was walking three Yorkshires. She said, "That's a cute puppy you've got. How old is it?"

I said, "Six."

She said, "Months?"

When I said years, she almost had convulsions. Then it was a miniature. It wasn't going to grow anymore? She had thought it was just a plump little puppy who would thin out and grow into a large standard. How did I let her get so fat? (Look, you run into at least three of these a day. This is one of the occupational hazards of walking a dog.)

"She's always had a weight problem," I explained. "However, in spite of everyone's concern, she's feeling great and hasn't been near a doctor in two years."

"You mean you don't take her in for a regular six-month checkup?"

I said I did not! And had no intentions of putting Josie through any needless probing. As a puppy this girl had gone through enough jabbing and examining to last her a lifetime. To this day, if we even pass the doctor's office she goes into a violent case of the shakes.

"But she's forty-two years old," the woman insisted.

Who was forty-two? Even Josephine look interested. Josephine was forty-two, the woman insisted. A dog's life is seven to our one. At six, Josie was forty-two. A middle-aged woman.

I rushed the middle-aged woman home and called Dr. White's office. They said yes indeed, she certainly was forty-two. Can you imagine what this did to me? I stared at the six-year-old baby who was happily chewing at one of my hair curlers and tried to see her in her true status—a mature matron! It was ridiculous. She was just a little girl.

Irving also made some inquiries on his own. Everyone verified the seven to one deal. No matter how we sliced it, Josephine was definitely forty-two. It was the first time I faced the awful realization—Josephine might not be with us forever!

I went into a stunned depression. Why were dogs given such a short life span? I once saw a sign in a pet shop: "The only love you can buy is the love of a puppy." It's so true! Once you take a puppy into your home, its only aim in life is to devote every waking second to you. Its only goal is to win your affection, please you, amuse you, and love you with a consistency that cannot be matched by any human's love. Because other than eating and sleeping, a dog lives only for his master. I'm not going to be one of those cranks who goes around hinting that dogs are nicer than people. I'm going to be one of those cranks who comes right out and says dogs *are* nicer than people!

But remember, I said nicer. Not more important, or more intelligent. If you are sick a dog can't dial the phone for the doctor, or spoon feed you a bowl of broth. He can't provide a home for you, raise your children, invent vaccines, become a lawyer, surgeon, or president. He isn't interested in the problems of civilization or the world. He's only interested in you. That's why he's nicer. He has to be. He is not harassed by any outside influences.

Take Irving for example. Irving loves me more than Josephine does. In an all-encompassing way. A practical way. Like most people who are in love with each other and their marriage, we are a unit that almost functions as one. We think as a unit—I can't picture any future without him and I can't remember any kind of a real life before him. I love his company, his sense of humor, his—well—you get the idea. I think he's the most sensational man in the world! And he has proven he feels the same way about me.

But when I wake in the morning, does Irving bounce up and cover my face with adoring kisses and shake with excitement and joy at the mere sight of me? Does he act like it's the seventh miracle that fate has permitted us to spend another day together? He does not! But Josephine does!

Irving's morning greeting varies. It depends on the hours of sleep he's had, or the appointments that loom on the coming day's agenda. If he's had seven hours of sleep and there's no imminent crisis ahead, he will greet me something like this:

"Did you put on the water for the coffee or do you want me to do it?"

But if he has not had a restful night, and the coming day is a blockbuster, his morning greeting will go something like this:

"How many times *did* you get up during the night? I heard you in the kitchen at least twice! I didn't sleep a wink because you were making such a racket." As I place the instant coffee before him with loving hands, he continues, "Have you changed the brand of coffee or have you just lost the magic knack again?"

However he begins to perk up after a shower, and by the time he is dressed he is almost his old romantic self. As he walks out of the door he tosses, "Well, take it easy. You walk her, I'm late! Bye. I love you."

I think I've stated my case for dogs. They are such nice people. And I reiterate: Why are they given such a short shake on life? Other animals get a better break. Look at the elephant. He lives for over a hundred years. And once they've cut his teeth out and made ivory doodads, what can an elephant do for you? Just eat peanuts and smell up the zoo. And take a turtle. He lives for centuries. Outside of being a pretty fair dish of soup, what has a turtle done for you lately?

Irving didn't take the idea of the seven to one span lightly either. He insisted a checkup for Josie was long overdue. And he even went along with the idea that it should be done with semiannual regularity.

I refused. Why subject her to the terror of the doctor's office when she was in such excellent health? Besides, maybe we would never have to face an existence without Josie, despite the fact that in four years she'd be seventy. After all, the atom bomb could drop any day! Then I decided we must put the seven-year bit out of our minds. We were getting maudlin. We should live and enjoy Josie for today. Irving agreed. But subconsciously he developed a new attitude toward Josie. Hysterical hypochondria!

He'd be reading the *Times*. Suddenly he'd put down the paper and stare at her. "Why is she breathing so hard?"

"Because she's been playing ball for an hour. Remember? You've been tossing it."

"But why is she breathing with her tongue hanging out?"

"Because she's been breathing that way since she was born. All dogs do."

Another time he yelled and said he felt a big lump in her chest. I dashed to feel the lump. It was a lump all right. A solid lump of fat!

However the real crisis came a few weeks later while we were lying in bed. We were doing what every normal, adjusted, happily married couple does in bed late at night. We were watching Jack Paar. Josie was industriously kissing Irving's face. Suddenly Irving said, "Jackie, I have an important statement to make."

I grew tense. After all, he had come up with this right in the middle of one of Alex King's most important stories.

"Now I don't want you to get upset," he explained. "What I am about to say is not personal. It's purely clinical."

I could hear my heart pounding as I waited.

"You know how I feel about Josie," he began tentatively. Meanwhile Josie shifted positions so she could lick the other side of his face.

My voice was shrill. "What about Josie?"

"Well, I hate to break this to you . . . but the girl's mouth does not exactly smell like a flower garden. For the first time I can see what Last-One was talking about."

I invited Josie over to kiss me. And I had to admit

he did have a point. Of course she could never offend me, but I could understand where someone with an overdeveloped smeller like Last-One's might find a basis for complaint.

After giving Josie's mouth a thorough inspection, Irving decided a good session with the dentist would straighten everything out. He said her teeth were just loaded with tartar. To me they looked like pearls, but this new member of the dental society insisted he saw tartar.

"Take her to the dentist tomorrow and have her teeth cleaned immediately."

I explained there were no dog dentists. Dr. White's office would have to attend to the matter.

"Then take her to Dr. White's tomorrow and have him clean them immediately."

I said, "*We'll* take her to Dr. White's tomorrow and have her teeth cleaned immediately."

He insisted he had a week loaded with important appointments. He didn't have one free hour. I said I'd wait until the following week when his schedule could allow him to accompany me on this safari.

He said he might be busy for several weeks, but if I wanted to sit around and let the girl's teeth rot away just because I was a coward, then that's the way it would have to be. Besides, what was the big deal? This wasn't as if she was going to get needles jabbed into her or anything like that. It would take the doctor just a few minutes to scrape the tartar off her teeth. He finished with, "And even I who am the world's biggest coward in a dentist's chair am not afraid to have my teeth cleaned."

Well, he got to me with that last remark. I am also a coward at the dentist's. But they do manage to clean my teeth without gas or Novocain. Perhaps he had a point. A little teeth cleaning wouldn't hurt her a bit.

So the following morning Josie and I set forth to visit the doctor. It was a lovely spring day but Josie began shivering as soon as we turned up the proper street. She hadn't been there in two years, but she recognized the street! This is the only miniature poodle endowed with both the memory and stomach of an elephant.

We walked into Dr. White's establishment. A strange doctor greeted us. "I haven't been here for two years," I explained. "You must be new here."

"Allow me to introduce myself," he said. "*I* am Dr. White."

I almost fainted from shock.

Dr. White studied her chart. He clucked a few times as he went over the pages and pages of her case history. "I see she's been with us since puppyhood. Sorry I never got to handle her personally, but all the members of my staff are excellent."

I said they certainly were, but naturally we were thrilled to have his personal attention this time. Then I went on to explain that she was in the best of health, but just needed a little tartar scraped off her teeth. He took out his stethoscope and listened to her heart.

"Her heart is fine," I explained. "It's her teeth I want you to examine."

He ignored me and began flexing the joints of her legs. He tapped her bones. He went up and down her spine. Ten minutes later I gently tapped him on the arm and explained I didn't mean to butt in, or tell him how to run his business, but he was examining the wrong end. It was her teeth we had come to see him about.

He said, "We'll get to that in due time. Meanwhile I'm giving her a thorough checkup. Her chart says she hasn't had a checkup in two years." Then he added conversationally, "She has infected anal glands." But when he began to poke around the great white belly he really got excited. He couldn't believe it. He put her on a scale. She weighed twenty pounds.

He said, "She's too fat."

I nodded.

"She's got to lose this fat. I've never seen a poodle

who accumulated it all in one spot like this one. I want her to lose six pounds immediately."

I promised that she would. But meanwhile, would he please look at her teeth. He would. But not until he packed her anal glands!

I was getting feverish. All this trouble and he hadn't even gotten to her teeth yet! The next thing I knew a syringe was up Josie. She let out a startled yelp and I almost fainted. Dr. White called in an attendant to assist him as I was no help in the Florence Nightingale department.

Next he inspected her ears. Well, this was something. At least it was a move in the right direction. "Don't you ever remove this extra hair?" he snarled as he happily pulled pieces of fur out of Josie's ears.

"No one ever told me to," I snarled back. "For six years she's had that fur in her ears and she's never complained. And as far as anal glands go, she's been very happy with them too!"

He ignored me as he was busy looking into her eyes with a light.

Well her eyes are her most beautiful feature. I relaxed. "You've got to admit," I said proudly, "that she has the most beautiful eyes of any poodle in the world." (I was also doing this for Josie's morale. After all, he had found fault with every part of her.)

"Not only are they velvet brown," I went on, "but in some lights, they are almost midnight blue."

"That's because she has the beginnings of cataracts," he announced.

I began to shake more violently than Josie. I was also eager to get my hands on Irving. Just because he had gotten a little finicky about her breath, she was winding up as a basket case! I should have ignored him and given her a few Sen-Sen. Who cared about her breath? She wasn't singing duets in the opera. She wasn't offending fellow office workers. And except for Last-One, it really hadn't hurt her social life at all.

Although Dr. White had displayed genuine interest

in her ears, belly, eyes, and rear, he didn't really come to life until he looked into her mouth.

Of course he had never seen such tartar. But that wasn't the exciting feature. "Look at this," he exclaimed, as he wiggled one of her big strong molars. "The worst case of pyorrhea I've ever encountered!"

I didn't want to see or hear any more. "Just clean them," I begged.

"Oh, I will." He studied her mouth intently. "But I'm afraid a few will have to go."

"But they're not decayed!"

"No, but the only way I can save her mouth is to remove the really bad ones and treat the gums. Then the others will tighten up. With proper treatment her mouth can be cured."

"But if you take out one tooth, won't the others get loose because of the space and the change in bite?" (My dentist had explained all this when he gave me a bill for a hundred dollars to cap a molar. A molar that I really felt I could have lived without, that could have been painlessly extracted for twenty dollars. But *my* dentist refuses to let me lose a single tooth.) I began to explain all this to Dr. White.

"It's different with a dog," he replied loftily. "Dogs only use their canine teeth. They never chew with molars."

"How many will you have to pull?"

"Can't say positively until I've cleaned her mouth."

"Give me a rough estimate."

"Maybe three or four."

I grabbed Josie and started for the door.

His next line stopped my flight. "If she doesn't have those teeth attended to, she'll go blind faster than she has to."

When I opened my eyes I was on the couch in his private office. The attendant brought me some water and after I revived, I grabbed Josie and stated that we were leaving immediately. (A suggestion with which Josie was in full accord.)

He sat down and with a great show of patience tried to explain the medical facts. "Mrs. Mansfield, no one actually knows just why cataracts form. It's a filming over the lens of the eye. Human beings can have operations and the cloudy lens can be removed. Glasses restore perfect vision. However, without glasses they cannot see. Since dogs cannot wear glasses, their cataracts are not operable. But cataracts *can* be held at bay. At this point, your dog's cataracts are just beginning to form. Our job is to hold them back so she will have sight the rest of her life. We can put her on vitamin A. Twenty-five thousand units a day. That might help. Keeping her teeth in good condition is an absolute must. It's my personal theory that with dogs, there is a definite relationship between bad teeth and cataracts."

"How many teeth did you say will have to go?" I knew this was no time to worry about her tooth paste smile, but I was looking for some reassurance.

"I told you, I can't definitely say until I've cleaned them. To clean them right, we have to put her under total anesthesia. I suggest you leave her here now, and we'll get on the job right away."

"Can I wait?"

He shook his head. "It will take us a good hour to clean them. And then there might be the extractions. Also she should remain and sleep off the anesthesia. I suggest you leave her overnight."

I phoned Irving for advice. Irving wasn't in. The decision had to be my own. I looked at Josie. Her stare shouted, "Don't trust this bum. Let's get the hell out of here and quick!"

But I knew he was right. After all, a man who's been in surgery every day for six years does not need to get his kicks pulling Josie's teeth.

So I agreed. I didn't dare look at Josie as I walked out. I knew she was staring at me as if I was the real Ilse Koch. Even so, she took it better than Irving!

"Just like that," he shouted, "you left her there! With a strange doctor you never saw in your life?"

"But he was *the* Dr. White!"

"But there are other doctors. Other opinions."

"But why should I subject her to the fright of other examinations? And why should I try another hospital? This hospital has pulled her through all her childhood illnesses. And this time I have Dr. White himself, the chief of staff."

He said he wouldn't care if it was Dr. Schweitzer. He wouldn't let *any* doctor pull three or four good teeth without getting another opinion. To get him off this kick I gave him a brief rundown of her other ailments.

He was in a state of shock. If he went along with a prognosis like this there were only two alternatives. Change doctors or change dogs!

For the rest of the evening he kept dropping little snide remarks about hysterical women who panic and rush into needless operations. Like having good strong white molars pulled.

Of course I reminded him of the time he called in six throat specialists within twenty-four hours when he merely had a common garden variety sore throat.

"But at least I got a lot of opinions," he shouted.

"But they were all the same!" I shouted louder. (I've been on the stage and learned to reach the second balcony.)

Oh, it went on and on, and we both said many clever things, but since they were all in the same vein I won't bother to record them for posterity. And it was in this pleasant fashion that we passed the entire evening.

24

That Certain Smile

THE following morning I arrived at Dr. White's just as they were opening shop. The attendant said Josephine was fine and they'd give her to me immediately. But first they gave me the bill. Twenty-five dollars!

I pay ten dollars to have my teeth cleaned and they're much larger than Josie's. But I wrote the check in silence. Next time I'd establish a rate. Especially if this was going to be done on a regular six-month basis.

Josephine was brought in, straining at the leash—her old frisky self. She was eager to get to me, but even more eager to make a beeline out of the place.

But Dr. White insisted on having a little chat with me first. I held the squirming Josephine and listened patiently to the familiar lecture on obesity and its dangers. He wanted to see her in three weeks. To check her weight loss.

I agreed and gave him my most charming smile because Josie really seemed in top form, considering her ordeal, and I was also aware that she smelled just like a listerine ad. (Now, Last-One would offend her!)

I gave the fragrant darling a small kiss on her head as Dr. White droned on and on about the perils of cholesterol and overweight. Josephine settled snugly in my arms, secure that no matter what happened, she was with me from here on. To reassure me of this trust, she gave me a radiant smile. I screamed! I didn't see a sign of a tooth!

Oh yes, Dr. White casually stated, there had been a few more bad teeth than he had expected. So he had extracted them.

"Like how many?" (I really didn't want to know, but I'm a masochist.)

"Sixteen."

"Sixteen! How many has she got left?"

That's when he gave me the medical double talk. Or maybe I was just too dazed to comprehend. But I got the idea that she still had her chewing molars, her eye teeth, and a few others here and there. And since she wore a mustache and beard, no one would notice if her mouth puckered a bit. Being a mental coward, I let him get away with these soothing words.

When I got home it took me an hour before I could gather the nerve to make a personal inspection. I placed Josie on the bed and opened her mouth. All those darling little front teeth in the bottom were gone! Just a vast expanse of clear pink gum except for a stray molar here and there. The top was even worse. The front teeth were all gone but one. Right in the dead center. Why he bothered to leave that one I'll never know. It certainly didn't enhance her smile. Her eye teeth were still intact and I caught a glimpse of a few shiny molars way back. But as far as appearances went, let's face it! This girl was toothless!

But I had no time to indulge in my own hysteria. I faced a much more serious crisis. Irving. How did I break this to him? I had to come up with something. Maybe a new poodle!

Or should I take the initiative and throw a small trauma. Go into screaming hysterics! Then he'd be so busy soothing me, I would escape without even a "How could you?"

Or should I play the hero? State that they wanted to pull all of her teeth. But I had refused. Singlehandedly I had fought the entire staff, and finally had made them settle for only sixteen! No, that wouldn't work.

Or maybe I should just say she's fine, and he'd never even notice anything was up—or out. After all, he didn't go around inspecting her mouth as a rule.

The more I thought about it, the more feasible it seemed. It was really the best course. Just say everything was great, and harp on the losing weight bit to get his mind off her mouth. And it worked—almost.

Irving came home and Josie bounced to the door to greet him. He was so delighted at her high spirits and quick recovery that it never occurred to him to give her a personal checkup. She smelled like a rose and was as playful as ever, and as the evening wore on, he began to grow quite extravagant with his praise of Dr. White. The guy must really know his stuff to put a dog through total anesthesia and pull a few teeth and have her back on her feet feeling no aftereffects in less than twenty-four hours! Why, when he had one wisdom tooth pulled, he had been in agony for three days. Maybe in the future we ought to let Dr. White take care of our teeth.

He rattled on, completely unaware of my unusual silence. And after he took her for her final walk of the evening, he sat on the bed to let her "help him" take off his socks.

This is their nightly ritual. He starts to pull a sock off, then she rushes in and gets a good grip on the toe part, and with much struggling and tug of war, she pulls it off. She is always very gentle and never nips a toe, but she has a marvelous time murdering the wool sock which becomes an imaginary foe.

Well, on this night Josie leaped forward as usual to pull. Of course the sock slid right out of her mouth. For a moment she sat and thought about it. Irving sat and thought about it too.

But Josie has an extremely high IQ, and in no time she had figured the solution. A side of the mouth attack was in order. After all, she still had the eye teeth and a few molars going for her. This worked fine except Irving almost lost a toe.

"What did they do?" he yelled. "Sharpen her teeth?"

Then he said, "Come to Daddy, Sweetheart. Daddy wants to inspect the pretty pearly teeth."

Naturally Sweetheart obeyed. Irving said, "Open the mouth so Daddy can see."

Sweetheart opened her mouth.

Daddy said, "Sweetheart, I've got to pull down your lips because I want to see the gorgeous front teeth." Daddy pulled down the lips.

Daddy said, "I must be doing something wrong. I swear I can't find her bottom teeth."

I said quietly, "There aren't any."

Then he found the one on top. Then he got out his glasses and made a thorough study. In a deadly tone he asked me how many teeth Sweetheart had left.

I said I hadn't made an actual count, but that sixteen were now in the possession of Dr. White.

Then I said, "Stop shouting! You're frightening Josie." He took a Seconal and said we'd discuss it in the morning.

The Seconal gave him nine hours of dreamless sleep. So when he awoke, it was one of his good mornings. He put on the water for the coffee. And when he saw Josie happily gum away at a piece of Sara Lee coffee cake he broke into a rapturous smile.

"Nothing can get our dog down. She doesn't *need* teeth. She's not even having trouble with the pecans!"

Naturally I didn't dare break the spell by announcing that the Sara Lee must go—and that the diet must return.

After all, I know enough to quit while I'm ahead!

25

It's *Not* What's Up Front That Counts

THE HISTORIC tooth extraction was followed by six happy uneventful months. Each night I shoved the vitamin A down her throat as Dr. White had prescribed. But we did not return for a checkup—I was afraid to—because Josie had not shed a single ounce. In fact she was now tipping the scales at twenty-two pounds. But every pound vibrated health and exhilaration. Maybe she puffed a bit after playing catch for an hour. But I am quite thin and *I* puff after five minutes in the sand trap at our golf course. So Josephine went along, enjoying life in her carefree gluttonous way. And that's how it went until one fine day in June.

Irving and Josie had gone for their usual morning stroll. Except that Irving came back with a worried look. Josie looked fine. He opened with that typical reassuring remark all husbands seem to come up with in time of peril.

"Now don't get excited, but something terrible just happened." This soothing remark got me hysterical before I even heard the news.

"We were in the park," he explained, "and she was giving her all to the hill and suddenly she let out a yelp."

"What kind of a yelp?"

"Just a quick yelp. Then everything was fine."

"Maybe she saw something that scared her."

"No. It wasn't a scared type of yelp."

"What kind of a yelp was it?"

His voice was exasperated. "I don't know. But today I won't go to the office. Instead I'll go to the sound library at NBC or CBS and listen to records of dog yelps. I won't leave until I find one that resembles hers. Then I'll phone you and tell you what type yelp it's labeled."

I said this was no time to get sarcastic. And he retaliated that he was not exactly a specialist in translating poodle yelps. Since Josie looked and acted okay, we decided there was nothing to do but wait until the next yelp occurred.

"But when it happens again, try and explain it better," I warned him.

"Oh sure! I'll take along my tape recorder!"

And so we watched and waited. When three yelpless days had passed, I began to think Irving had imagined the entire situation. Every time I took her to the park she performed in silent perfection.

On the fourth day we were walking down Central Park South when she suddenly felt the urge. Right in front of the Hampshire House! I tried to coax her across the street to the park, but she wouldn't budge. She ran right to the curb in front of the Hampshire House and went into that accordion-like position which means serious business.

The doorman gave me a withering stare. An incident like this is a real catastrophe to a hotel doorman —in the financial department. After all, when a doorman rushes to open the door of a cab, it is not because he gets his kicks playing Sir Galahad. His real thrill is the silver quarter that is placed in his palm for this gigantic service. But when a lady all gussied up in open-toed pumps steps forth from her cab and sinks her tootsies into a pile of you-know-what, she is apt to get a little unnerved. Unnerved enough to forget to give our pal the doorman his silver quarter. Sympathetic to anyone trying to make an honest buck, I try to co-operate with all doormen.

But Josie looks at it in a different light. She knows that in this life you must follow certain rules and regulations. And she follows the rules and regulations that apply to her. But as far as she's concerned, the doormen can look out for themselves. They have their own homes and their own bathrooms. And the rules of the New York Sanitation Department state the curb is her bathroom. *Any* curb. The signs say, "Curb Your Dog." They do not say, "Curb your dog, but not in front of the Hampshire House, Navarro, Pierre, or Sherry Netherlands." As a tax-paying citizen (after all she plunks down three dollars every year for her license plate) she figures she has a right to pick her curb. And even though she usually confines her activity to Central Park, once in awhile she gets bored with all the grass and trees and likes to liven things up by giving her business to a classy "name" hotel.

So there we stood. Josephine in her accordion position, the glaring doorman, plus ten autograph hunters who were waiting for Lucille Ball.

And then it happened! Josephine let out a yelp! I knew I hadn't imagined it because the doorman and the ten autograph hunters came over to see what was up.

But Josephine was still in action. And in the midst of her labors, she let out another yelp. This one was almost soprano in tone. And as she continued with the business at hand she kept accompanying it with piercing little squeals.

I didn't know what to do! I couldn't drag her away until she had finished. I was not only sick with worry, but unbearably embarrassed. The function itself is delicate enough without the added attraction of *La Traviata*.

Say what you will about this being a natural func-

tion of nature—but no one ever quite carries it off
with unperturbed composure. If you don't believe me,
catch the expression of someone who is standing with
a dog who is curbing itself. The owner stands there
with a look of nonchalance he does not feel—even
though he tells himself he is doing nothing more than
holding the leash. But no matter how you slice it, he
is still part of the act! And feels it. It seems to be the
one unsolved problem of dog etiquette. The book tells
you how to act on every occasion but this.

Of course on this particular day people had a right
to stare. Just as I was about to ask the doorman to
call for an ambulance, Josie came to an abrupt finish
and gaily leaped back on the pavement, happy as a
lark, completely unaware that she had caused a minor
sensation on Central Park South.

For as her yelps had continued, many interested
spectators had joined our group. And don't forget,
for openers we began with the ten Lucille Ball autograph hunters and the irritated doorman. Of course
they didn't just stand there. They offered helpful suggestions. Like "Hey, what's up?" or "Lady, do you
know your dog is hollering?" One woman was positive we were all on "Candid Camera."

The moment we reached the privacy of our apartment, I poured myself a stiff drink and put in a frantic
call to Irving. Usually I can never locate Irving when
I am in the middle of a crisis with Josie. And this was
no exception. His secretary had no idea when he
would return.

I called Bea Cole. I chose her over Joyce because
Joyce was already working on her third dog to my
one, and I was beginning to feel maybe she was a little
hard on dogs. But Bea had once nursed an ailing Af-
ghan back to robust health, and her mother had reared
two cocker spaniels from puppyhood into senility.
(I didn't call Dr. White because my nerves were too
frayed to face a lecture on her weight.)

Bea suggested hot sitz baths along with those miracle suppositories that everyone takes as a sure cure (before he gives up and eventually has the operation). I tried the sitz baths and the miracle suppositories on Josie, who submitted to these ministrations with an air of martyrdom. Like, she didn't know what the hell was going on—but if I was enjoying myself, she'd manage to put up with it. In spite of my handiwork, Josephine yelped at least once a day.

Finally, after a particularly embarrassing session in front of Saks, I announced to Irving that we would have to make the trek to Dr. White's. And when I said *we*, I meant *we* as all-inclusive.

So bright and early the next morning, Josephine, Irving, and I arrived at Dr. White's. Once again the miracle happened. We were received by Dr. White himself. After listening to our saga of the yelps, he put her on the table and poked about a bit.

Then he announced, "This dog has infected anal glands."

"You told me that six months ago, Dr. White."

He gave me a vacant stare. Out came the long syringe. "I'm going to pack them."

This time there was an edge to my voice. "You also did that six months ago, Dr. White." (It was beginning to dawn on me that maybe he didn't recognize Josie.)

Irving whispered as assurance, "Jackie, he sees so many dogs every day." (Obviously the idea was beginning to dawn on Irving as well.)

"But no dog looks like Josie," I whispered back. "How could he forget her?"

Irving is more realistic. "It's her face and personality that no one forgets. And let's face it, at this moment he is not exactly staring into her glorious eyes!"

I calmed down a bit. Irving did have a point.

Finally he looked at her exquisite face. He said conversationally, "This dog has the beginning of cataracts." (He was an old man so I didn't hit him! Besides, Irving was holding my arms.)

Then he looked into her mouth and said, "Oh, I see she's had some teeth extracted."

That did it! Even Irving was outraged! All right, we'll concede he sees a lot of dogs. He might not recognize her anal glands. But when he personally had extracted sixteen teeth from that magnificent face and didn't recognize her, well, that finished him with us!

It's not that I'm prejudiced. Everyone says she has an unusual face. And if Dr. White couldn't remember that face, well, it was high time we found a doctor who would. And so I began shopping for another physician.

26

Narrowing Down the AMA

It isn't easy to find a new doctor. And there's only one way. Just ask around. Since all my friends who owned dogs used my doctor, I had to do my asking around among total strangers. And this method is not without certain occupational hazards. Because you just can't walk up cold to a person with a dog and say, "Who's your doctor?" I don't know why, but you can't.

There's a definite preliminary, called small talk. First you pass the time of day. You comment on the charming personality of the dog you meet and find out the age of the dog. If the dog is five or under then the whole thing has been a waste of time. Just nod and go in search of another dog. But if you run into one that's ten or twelve and is still navigating, you're home! This is pay dirt!

But can you say, "Who is your vet?" Get the address, and let it go at that? No, you cannot. Even after the small talk is established, there is more groundwork to be done. You've got to listen to the entire medical history of the ancient survivor—and act interested. You must keep fading the owner with an occasional "You don't say!" or "How about that!"

I almost froze to death in Central Park as I listened to the intimate details of a fourteen-year-old standard poodle's hysterectomy! I tched tched right down to

171

the last stitch, then with my pencil poised I finally asked the name of this miraculous surgeon. The woman bristled. "Don't dare use *him!* He gave my poor Minnie peritonitis! In the middle of the night we had to rush her to Dr. Carr in Brooklyn for an emergency operation. She was fed intravenously for two weeks, and Dr. Carr had to remove a kidney, but she made it. Didn't you, Minnie baby?"

Well, Brooklyn was a little out of the way, but to me distance was no deterrent to secure the services of a doctor of such caliber. I asked the address of the marvelous Dr. Carr.

"Oh, he died three months ago," the woman answered. "By the way, who's your vet? I'm in the market for a specialist myself."

In spite of many such backbreaking incidents, I did manage to accumulate a list. A list of sworn specialists. Yet there was not one in whose hands I was willing to place my full confidence or Josephine. You see, every success story was matched by an equal tale of disaster. Take Dr. X who had pulled little Geronimo through intestinal flu. Geronimo's owner was willing to build a shrine to this Dr. X. Sounds pretty good, right? Down goes Dr. X's address and phone number. But one block later I run into a lady who shrieks that this same Dr. X put her little Cocoa to sleep needlessly. Go to Dr. Y; he was the only doctor. Sure, except the day before two people had told me Dr. Y was a butcher.

Finally a friend of mine, a born poodle nut, who owns a gorgeous gray poodle named Sam told me about Dr. Raphael. And Yvette Schummer (Sam's mother) was absolutely definite when she stated he was the best doctor in the world. The next day Lee Reynolds confirmed this opinion. Dr. Raphael took care of Moppet and Moppet had two years on Josie. And the more I asked around, the more Dr. Raphael became the magic word.

Dr. Raphael's hospital is situated in a brownstone

house in the West Sixties. He and his associate, Dr. Bernard run the entire establishment. I rushed Josie there for a thorough checkup. Needless to say I made Irving accompany me on this all-important expedition.

The examination brought on the usual discourse on her weight. They agreed with the absent-minded Dr. White about her anal glands. But they kept reiterating that she *must* lose weight! Immediately! Then I was presented with a tube with a nozzle. I stared at it. So did Josie.

Dr. Raphael explained that a daily injection for one month would polish off the squealing problem. Then both he and Dr. Bernard went into another tirade about her weight. They demanded to see her at the end of a month—five pounds lighter!

Irving, who can be very two-faced, sat there in complete agreement with the doctors. But the moment we were out of the door he turned to me and said, "Of course you realize the tube and nozzle job is strictly *your* department!"

"My department! Why should she hate me? We'll take turns!" He absolutely refused.

But Josephine didn't hate me. She just thought I was a little peculiar. Every time I came near her I was either shoving a vitamin down her throat or a tube up her rear. And to top these indignities, I was getting very stingy with the Yummy handouts. The payment for taking a vitamin had always been two Yummies. She figured a jab up the *derrière* was worth at least double the amount. Instead she just got a pat on the head and a small piece of rye crisp.

I stuck to the tube and the diet for ten days until Irving came up with a counter suggestion.

"Look, Dr. Raphael said the tube bit would be over in a month. Meanwhile, this dog is having a hard time finding one redeeming feature about you. Not only does she privately think you've suddenly become some kind of a degenerate with all the attention you're giving her rear end, but to top everything, you're starving

her to death. She's been overweight for seven years.
One more month isn't going to kill her. Let's get the
homemade Dr. Kildare treatments over with, then
we'll go in for the Elizabeth Arden streamlining
routine."

I decided Irving's idea made sense. So did Josephine.
So we went back to the Sara Lee and the good life,
and Josie began to look at me as if I was slowly re-
gaining my senses. Of course in her opinion I still
clung to a few little eccentricities, but she was positive
I'd soon make a complete recovery.

At the end of the month, the tube and the yelping
became things of the past. Unfortunately, so did the
diet.

27

The Heiress

Nᴇᴇᴅʟᴇss to say, we did not return to Dr. Raphael's at the end of the month. The screeching had stopped, but Josie's great white belly was still in evidence. I needed a few weeks to slim her down. After all, it had taken a good deal of research to acquire such a fine doctor, and I didn't want to lose him. And he had been more concerned with her diet than her *derrière*.

A month passed, but Josie remained her chubby, happy self. And when another month passed and everything seemed fine (except her diet) I decided Dr. Raphael could wait a little longer. So could her diet.

It was summer and we had to go back to the Coast for a few weeks. The traumatic windup of Josie's sojourn with Last-One had taught me a good lesson: the advantages of paying one's way. Unfortunately courtesy and respect which are hard to gain, can often be bought. A person who checks into a hotel and generously tips the staff, is always welcomed back with beaming good will. When he leaves, he is practically carried to his cab by a convulsively happy bellboy, who pleads, "Now don't be a stranger. Please visit us soon again!"

Now I ask you, does your Aunt Emma act that way after you have spent a week at her place in the country? You know she doesn't, unless you are a Texas oilman and she is your only living heir and has seen your will. I am not bitter. Just realistic. If the great

American dollar works better than charm, who am I to be a pioneer?

Josie goes along with this thinking too. Besides, she's a "result player." I mean, if someone gives her Yummies or rubs her belly, she's not concerned whether the reaction comes from the heart or the pocketbook. Just so long as it comes.

So she was perfectly happy to trade in Last-One for Mr. Ingram and his "paid" attentions—Mr. Ingram who welcomed her with open arms and raved about her charm and personality. So you can imagine my consternation when I dialed Mr. Ingram to give him the glorious news that once again his house guest would be en route, and Mr. Ingram's phone did not answer. I called every hour on the hour. After three days it became obvious that this time Mr. Ingram was someone else's house guest.

Joyce immediately volunteered to take Josie. After all, she had tons of experience with dogs. There had been Toulouse, then Tony—then there was Baby Doll. Yes, I said there *was* Baby Doll. One day, out of the blue, Baby Doll just picked up and died with no warning. This is a very frustrating thing for a dog to do to an owner. At least if a dog gives out with a small warning—like a convulsion or two—then the owner can rush around to specialists. He can beat his chest in despair and receive condolences from sympathetic friends. I mean, it's only fair that a dog warns you when he has intentions of departing from this world. It gives you a chance to worry, to mourn, and to receive sympathy. But when a dog just goes off and dies without any warning, the owner is left with egg on his face. Instead of sympathy, friends come up with hostile inquiries. "What did you do? He looked fine yesterday." And you have to justify his sudden demise. A thing like this can leave you with a real guilt complex. Joyce began to feel she just didn't have a green thumb where dogs were concerned.

And she's so good to dogs. Baby Doll might have had a short life, but Baby Doll lived! She started life in Billy's mansion on East Ninety-third Street. She spent her weekends on an island in Darien. And when Joyce and Billy decided to get a divorce, Baby Doll sat in on all the fascinating negotiations. When Joyce fled to Switzerland to put Vicki in school, recover from her divorce, and sit on an Alp to think things over, who sat on that Alp with her? Baby Doll.

When Joyce grew bored with the Alps, she and Baby Doll gave Paris and Rome a whirl. And then, without giving any notice, Baby Doll upped and died.

Another girl might have tossed in the towel. But Joyce is made of sterner stuff. She decided to have another go at a French poodle. She bought one in Switzerland. A tiny ball of black fluff with an immense pedigree. She wrote me ecstatic letters. This was it! Josie had a new cousin. His name was Micky. The months passed and the glowing reports continued. Micky, unlike Toulouse was growing all in one piece. He was perfectly formed.

A few months later the reports were less enthusiastic. Micky was still a beauty. But Micky was also still growing. And then came the final blow. Micky was a standard. Joyce gave him to a lovely Swiss family and returned to New York dogless. She also remarried Billy. And as a wedding present, Billy presented her with an adorable toy Yorkshire. It weighed two pounds and its name was Esther.

Esther lived for ten glorious action-packed days. Even the autopsy couldn't show any good reason for Esther's sudden fadeout. And now that Joyce was between dogs, she insisted on taking Josie while we were away.

Now you've got to admit I was in a spot. Joyce had gone through five dogs to my one. To hand over Josie was like signing Josie's execution sentence. To refuse would end a beautiful friendship. Irving solved it all by telling Joyce he had given Bea Cole a contract to take care of Josie.

Joyce was bewildered. "What do you mean a contract?"

"Remember when Bea worked for me as a chaperone to contestants on one of my shows?"

Joyce remembered.

"Well, this time I hired her as chaperone for Josie at fifty dollars a week." (Irving's nose was twitching as it always does when he ad libs or lies outrageously.) But Joyce doesn't know about Irving's nose, so it went over very well with her. Now all we had to do was break the news to Bea.

Naturally Bea was eager to take Josie. But she refused the money. When we explained the situation in detail, she smiled, but spurned our offer. Josie was a welcome house guest.

Then I pointed out the saga of Last-One. That did it. Bea and I have been like sisters, and she had no desire to change the relationship. But as she put it, where Josie was concerned, I was like a nut and overly sensitive. And aside from any personal feelings about me, she happened to be crazy about Josie on her own, and if the only way she could get Josie was as a contractual employee, okay. She'd drag out the good china and take Josie on as a well-paying house guest.

Irving actually drew up a contract and handed it over to Bea, along with Josie, her Yummies, her squeak toys, and vitamin A. Bea promised detailed letters on Josie's activities. Since we weren't sure how long we'd be away, Irving said he'd mail the check each week.

Within a week of our departure, we received the first letter.

June 10th

Dear Jackie,

I have not broken it to Roby (Bea's husband) or Karen, that the girl is an heiress and is a paying house guest. I figured it might change their whole attitude toward her. You know how self-conscious some people get when they're around millionaires. Overly polite and overly courteous. This way Roby and Karen still treat her just like one of us, and I figure it's better for Josie too. No sense getting the girl spoiled just because she's got a buck.

Everything is going just fine. We had one small incident the other day. Josie and I were strolling along Fifth Avenue, when along came one of those water wagons that clean the street. Before we had a chance to jump, it hit us full blast. I only got slightly damp, but Josie who was nearest to the curb, got drenched. And what got me so mad was the attitude of all the pedestrians. They burst out laughing. Josie was so furious about the soaking that she refused to budge. She stood there, immovable, livid and dripping. What was I to do? Let her catch pneumonia? Naturally no cab would take us. In her dripping state she might soil their upholstery. I don't know why, but when cab drivers see you with a slightly damp dog, they suddenly act as if their torn plastic seats are handmade needle point.

So there we were on Fifth Avenue—dripping wet. And one of us was a very rich dog who was forking over fifty bucks a week for services rendered. So I figured to hell with my new black silk dress! I picked her up and carried her the ten blocks home. Then I rubbed her dry with a turkish towel and she was completely happy.

Have a nice time and relax. Everything is fine.

Love,
Bea

P.S. What is the name of that fancy cleaner on Madison Avenue who charges twenty dollars to clean a dress? My cleaner refuses to touch the black dress.

June 17th

Dear Jackie,

Forget about the dress. The fancy Madison Avenue cleaner can't fix it either, but Roby said it wasn't too flattering on me anyway. And stop worrying about Josie's diet. Of course we are following it. To make sure you don't accuse me of adding any excess poundage on the little flower, we had an official weighing in contest the day she arrived. I don't know how you weigh her, but I have my own system. I get on the scale and weigh myself. Then I take Josie on with me and figure the additional weight for Josie. When we got on the scale I was wearing curlers and a light summer dress. Josie was nude. I weighed one hundred and twenty pounds. Josie weighed twenty-three pounds.

Your check arrived. Thank you very much. I still haven't told Roby or Karen.

Love,
Bea

June 22nd

Dear Jackie,

The secret is out! Roby accidentally opened the letter from Irving thinking it was some new piece of advice on the care and feeding of Josie. Naturally, out fell the check. At first he was furious. How dare I accept money from Josie. But I dragged out the contract and explained everything.

All I can say is Roby now looks at Josie in a new light. He stares at her with a faraway look in his eyes. He says, "Why should I kill myself being an engineer? Flying back and forth to Birmingham, jeopardizing my life in planes. All I need is three more poodles like Josie, and I've got it made. I can retire."

And as I predicted everything *has* changed. His attitude toward her is that of a rich relative. At cocktail time when I slip her some *pâté*, he yells, "Stop that! Do you want to give her cholesterol? We've got to keep this girl alive a long, long time. After all, Jackie and Irving travel a lot. This isn't just a dog—it's an annuity."

When Karen throws Josie the ball, Roby grabs it and roars, "Are you crazy? Do you want her to have a heart attack?"

Even my mother has gotten into the act. She now goes out of her way to rub Josie's belly and makes snide little remarks to Josie like: "Josie, *I* live in Carmel. It's country there. I bet you'd like it better than this old city apartment. Why don't you tell your Daddy and Mommy that you'd love to stay with Aunt Amy next time."

And it's even rubbed off on Karen. The other day Josie and I were out for two hours. When we returned Karen was frantic. "Where has she been?" (Not where had *I* been! She wasn't at all concerned about me.) I said I had to pick up a few of her camp things at Bloomingdale's. Karen turned white. "You took Josie to Bloomingdale's! With all those people? She might catch a virus!"

The party's over. Josie is no longer treated like family. Everyone stares at her like she is a blue chip stock—paying better dividends than AT&T or IBM.

Love,
Bea

July 2nd

Dear Jackie,

We invested in an air conditioner for the bedroom. We have one in the living room, but at night Josie likes to sleep with us in the bedroom, and it's too hot in there for her. She begins to pant and choke around two A.M. We kept putting her in the living room where it was nice and cool but she was lonely. So we got a one-ton unit for the bedroom. It's been in for three days and Josie adores it.

Of course we have to sleep under blankets, and

Roby is running a slight fever along with his chest cold, but we have to consider Josie. After all, she's a paying guest and is entitled to the best.

Love,
Bea

July 11th

Dear Jackie,

When you write, write to the address of the hotel on the letterhead. Our apartment building is having the halls painted, and Josephine just couldn't stand the odor of paint. We thought she was going to faint. So Roby and I checked into this hotel for a few days. It's a lovely hotel, and of course we took a suite that is air conditioned, so I want you to know she's perfectly comfortable. Roby's cold is better, and the doctor says his bursitis will go away if he just remembers not to turn during the night and let the air conditioning hit his right shoulder.

Love,
Bea

P.S. Next weekend we're taking her with us when we go to visit Karen in camp. I called the camp and they're delighted that Josephine is coming along. Of course they can't let us stay at their lodge for the weekend as they don't allow dogs. But they've found us a perfectly marvelous motel only sixty miles from the camp. Now don't you worry, what's a little drive back and forth each day. Roby just loves to drive.

Love,
Bea

July 20th

Dear Jackie,

Camp was fine. Josie loved it. But you forgot to tell me Josie gets car sick on any extended drive. But think nothing of it. The car is two years old and needed to be reupholstered anyway.

Love,
Bea

August 2nd

Dear Jackie,

The other day when Josie and I were taking a walk down Park Avenue, she stopped at the curb to "you-know-what." Suddenly she let out a yelp. I almost fainted. Partly from fright and partly from the closeness of the crowd that gathered round us. I rushed her over to Dr. Raphael. Doll, you forgot to tell me this had happened before. Dr. Raphael seemed very nonchalant about it. In fact he seemed more concerned about her weight. He gave me a real blasting—as if this little flower had come to me with a wasp waistline, and maybe I had done all the damage. Then he sent us home with stern orders about dieting. He also presented me with a darling little tube and nozzle. I asked him what I was to do with it. He told me! Three times a day for a week!

Love,
Bea

P.S. By the way, when *are* you coming home?

28

Josephine's Private Life

Anyone doing a character analysis on Josephine would have to rate her pretty high. Her nature is kind and loving. Her disposition is cheerful and sparkling. But being human, she has one tiny fault. She doesn't understand about sharing.

Anything that belongs to her is hers! Anything that belongs to me is also hers. For example, it's an unwritten agreement that we go halfies on anything I eat. I have two hands. One I can use as I like. The other must toss her ball or rub her belly.

Perhaps something traumatic happened in her early childhood before she came to us. Who knows? Maybe at feeding time, when her Mama rolled over, Josie didn't get a fair shake at the refreshment pump. Or maybe she got one that ran dry. Or maybe it was Mama herself who showed no particular love or devotion. After all, Josie's papers claim that Mama was quite a champion. She was always prancing around the show ring, coming home with cups and blue ribbons. Now any psychiatrist will tell you that a mother who is constantly in the limelight often breeds some kind of psychosis in her offspring. Maybe Josie's sisters and brothers are all hopeless neurotics and Josie's marvelous outgoing personality saved her from any real psychosis, except for this minor vice—a streak of extreme possessive selfishness.

It's such a small fault, I shouldn't even mention it. I mean, I really can exist without sharing half her
184

Yummy or being invited to have a go at her marrow bone. But she also refuses to share her social life. And as I've stated, everyone who knows me, knows Josephine. But everyone who knows Josephine does *not* know me!

And Josephine knows Greta Garbo, Laurence Harvey, Margaret Leighton, Michael Rennie, Nat King Cole, Rudolph Bing, and Richard Burton.

She wouldn't have even noticed Garbo if it hadn't been for me! We were walking down Fifty-seventh Street when I spotted the familiar dark glasses and slouch hat. I said, "Look Josie, that's Greta Garbo." (See what I mean? I share all my experiences with her.)

When Garbo drew near, Josie stopped and sniffed a small greeting. Miss Garbo leaned down and said, "Well, hello there." Josie smiled at Garbo. Garbo smiled at Josie. I puckered up, waiting for Josie to extend herself and draw me into the picture. But no, I stood there like a lump—an inanimate object at the other end of the leash, while Garbo and Josie exchanged all kinds of little pleasantries. Then Garbo, without even a glance at me, went on her way, and Josie with equal nonchalance, tugged me off in the opposite direction.

The case of Laurence Harvey and Margaret Leighton was even more inexcusable. At the time, Margaret Leighton was starring in a play called *Separate Tables*. She was married to Laurence Harvey and they had an apartment directly across the hall from us. The hotel endowed everyone on our floor with the services of a delightful Irish maid. This gem of old Erin and I struck up an immediate friendship. We had so much in common. We both adored Josie and hated the housekeeper. She told me wonderful stories about the old country and sold me sweepstake and lottery tickets by the score. In fact this leprechaun could do everything but clean, but her sparkling personality coupled with her devotion to Josie, kept me from requesting a replacement. I merely hired my own personal maid to help keep things clean, which in no way insulted this flower of Killarney. In fact, her attitude implied that I had hired a companion for her. She not only took her morning coffee with Evie, my maid, but converted Evie into another customer for the sweepstakes and lottery deals. Unfortunately, one fine day, this dear Irish maid had one moment of truth with the housekeeper, and is no longer with us.

However, at the time when she was brightening our lives (if not the apartment) she was one of Josie's most intimate companions. Unbeknown to me, Josie usually accompanied her on her rounds, when she made a stab at cleaning the other apartments on our floor. Of course these excursions never took place when I was home (maybe deep down the pixie had an idea I wouldn't approve) but since I was out at least three or four afternoons a week, Josephine managed to enjoy a pretty ~~ ..~ive social life.

The first inkling I got of Josie's "Hi neighbor" policy, was with Margaret Leighton and Laurence Harvey. Josie and I were standing waiting for the elevator when the door across the hall opened, and out came the Harveys. They didn't notice me. I'm only five foot six and a half in my stocking feet. Josie is one foot, three inches when she stands on her hind legs. But they saw her.

Two beautiful English accents pealed out a simultaneous greeting, "Josephine dahling. How are you today?"

"Dahling" gave them a fervent tail wag, reserved only for real buddy-buddies.

"Dahling, we missed you at breakfast this morning."
Breakfast? I had never even made it for a get-to-know-you sherry. Josephine rolled over on the floor so Mr. Harvey could rub her belly. Miss Leighton chuckled with delight. During this entire social exchange I stood like the invisible man.

The following morning I had a slight discussion

with the leprechaun. I began with breakfast at the
Harvey's. Oh it didn't happen every day, I was assured. But sometimes when she and Josie went in to
make up the beds, the Harvey's were having breakfast.
Naturally they'd invite Josephine to join them. Josie
just adored that wee spot of bacon or perhaps a wee
bit of a biscuit.

I did five minutes on the "wee spot of bacon and
wee bit of biscuit." Poodles are not supposed to eat
bacon. Then I explained about Josie's figure problem.
I didn't mind her enlarging Josephine's social horizon
with the visits to other apartments, but I didn't want
to enlarge Josie's already ample measurements. I extracted a solemn promise that not one morsel of food
would go down Josie's throat without my consent.

And the leprechaun was a woman of her word. The
following day I found a note saying, "I looked in the
Harvey's refrigerator and saw a batch of Canadian
bacon. That will probably be tomorrow's breakfast.
Does Canadian bacon agree with the little darlin'?"

After the unfortunate incident with the housekeeper,
the pride of Erin was replaced by an uncommunicative
but dedicated cleaner from Jamaica, so Josie's social
life came to a sudden end. I don't know how she managed to meet Michael Rennie. But after the Harveys
moved out, Mr. Rennie moved in, and one day, as we
stood waiting for the elevator, there he was, just like
his predecessors, greeting Josie and ignoring me.

Richard Burton followed Michael Rennie. He only
remained a short time and was extremely busy. But he
found time to meet Josephine. One day he gave her a
little scratch on the ear as we waited for the elevator.
The elevator took a long time in coming, and I could
swear, he almost noticed me. If Josephine had made
the slightest attempt, I'm sure a proper introduction
could have been performed. But instead she gave him
the shiv paw, which meant "continue with the rubbing until the elevator comes." And after all, when a
man is bending down rubbing a dog's ear, it is hard

to come up with any proper introductory small talk.

And when we parted, she gave him the usual phoney tail wag. If he only knew—*I'm* the one who plays his *Camelot* album. Josie prefers *West Side Story*.

I finally met an occupant of the apartment across the hall—a lovely lady named Mary Mayer. Naturally Josie got to know her first, but Mary became one of my good friends. Through no help from Josie. Mary has a dachshund named Baby. And Baby performed the introduction!

29

The Tragedy

IT WAS a day like any other day. Josie and I had been to the park. When we returned she rushed me to the kitchen to demand her payoff—a Yummy, because she had taken a nice walk in Central Park on a brisk November day, and had performed in the manner intended.

As I reached for the Yummy and she heard the wonderful sound of the box rattling, she danced ahead of me into the bedroom. (She always eats in bed.) Drooling, she leaped on the bed to await her treat. Only she didn't make it.

I had noticed that she needed a longer running start to make the leap to the bed. Previously she had sprung on and off it as if it was a trampoline. When I had brought this fact to Irving's attention, he had shrugged and said if the jump got too high, we could always saw off the legs of the bed.

But this time she actually didn't make it. She was about two inches short. She slid to the floor awkwardly and let out a piercing scream. I leaped to her side and tried to find the injured part. She continued to scream and sob like a terrified child.

In moments of real disaster, I go icy calm. And this was a moment of real disaster! Especially when she turned down the Yummy I offered as an attempt to sooth her. I fought back my own panic as she continued to screech. I sat on the floor and rubbed her tummy. Funny how odd pieces of information come to you in moments like these. I dimly remembered that when someone is hit by a car you don't move them. You let them remain on the street until an ambulance arrives. So with one hand rubbing her head, I crawled on the floor and tried to stretch to reach the phone to call Dr. Raphael. I couldn't quite make it.

Suddenly Josephine stopped yelping, shook herself, stood up with a look of, "What's up, Doc?" I began to breathe again. And when she gobbled up the Yummy that lay on the floor, even my heart resumed its normal beat. Then she began to walk. Only she walked on three legs. She held up her back right hind leg. If anything, this gave me some reassurance. At least she hadn't broken her back. And I also knew that if an animal drags its leg, it's broken. When they hold it up it usually means a sprain or strain.

I called Irving and told him about the accident. For once, the "Absolute Authority" agreed with my analysis. In fact he advised me against calling the doctor. She only got nervous when she went to the doctor's. She had gone through enough as it was with the sprain. Besides, as a boy he had seen millions of dogs skipping around Brooklyn on three legs. She'd be her old self by the time he got home.

In a way he was right. She was as sparkling as ever in the evening, except she sparkled on three legs. But neither her appetite or spirit seemed impaired and she was obviously in no pain so I held back the panic.

But when four days went by and she seemed completely satisfied to go through life on three legs, I felt some action had to be taken. She was also keeping us up half the night. It was her habit to turn in when she was finally assured that all action for the evening was really over. This meant all lights out and both of us in bed. Then she went under the bed with a clear conscience and went to sleep herself. After an hour or so, the cold air from the open window seeped under the bed and caused her to change sleeping quarters. This was easily accomplished by springing to my bed and snuggling in my arms. But not on three legs!

Brilliant dog that she was, she had already mastered a beautiful three-point "leap down." But leaping up required four legs. Therefore, when it got too frigid under the bed, much as she hated to disturb us, it was a necessary action. She was very polite about it and had figured out an ingenious method. Nothing gauche like a bark. A bark would startle us. She'd hobble out from under the bed and stand beside my side of the bed for about five minutes, trying to get to me with a concentrated stare. (You'd be surprised how you can wake from a deep sleep when a small three-legged poodle keeps staring at you.) But if I slept through the stare, she'd hobble over to Irving's side and try it on him. If she batted double zero, she tried a small scratch on the arm with the shiv paw. And if this failed, she came up with a few little annoyed murmurs. One of us, in a half-conscious state, would lean over and pick her up. She'd reward us with a few grateful kisses and then settle down to sleep. This would not have been too disconcerting if that had been her only plans for the night.

Previously I had been dimly aware that at some time during the night Josie sprang into my arms. I also knew that at some point she returned to the floor. And then invariably wound up back in my arms in the morning. But I had never actually clocked her nocturnal activities. Now I had no choice. I was part of them.

It seems that after the first half hour of snuggling, our little princess gets too warm. This is remedied by traveling to the foot of the bed. Ten minutes later, obviously forgetting about the cold breezes that had wafted under the bed, this suddenly becomes the only appealing spot in town. Off she goes, on her own steam (courtesy of the three-point landing) to her haven under the bed. After ten minutes the goose bumps get to her, and a return engagement to our bed is in order. But she cannot jump up. This calls for another session of deep staring, pawing, and squeaking. And once again one of us reaches out and lifts her onto the bed.

And that's how it went. Night after night. We tried keeping the windows closed. This worked fine. She remained under the bed. But we almost suffocated.

I called Dr. Raphael. Dr. Bernard answered the phone. I explained about her sprain. Perhaps he could suggest a mild sleeping pill for her, until her leg healed.

He asked who had diagnosed it as a sprain. I told him all about my knowledge of sprains. Then he told me a few things. One of them was to bring her in immediately.

Both doctors were waiting for me. I tried to tell them it was nothing to be alarmed about, and if it weren't for her gymnastics during the night, I never would have bothered them.

They ignored me and studied Josie's leg.

"She feels marvelous otherwise," I insisted.

They didn't seem to hear me. "Let's hold off the X-rays for a week," Dr. Raphael told Dr. Bernard. Dr. Bernard nodded. They returned the patient to my waiting arms.

Dr. Bernard said, "You know, if she had been thinner, she would not have slipped."

Dr. Raphael said, "If she isn't walking normally within one week, bring her back. Meanwhile, put her on a diet."

Dr. Bernard looked at Dr. Raphael as if he hadn't heard right. "Put her on a diet!" His glance toward me implied that he secretly thought Irving and I got our kicks stuffing this dog. Then he said to Dr. Raphael, "I have warned these people about her weight over and over. It's almost a lost cause."

Obviously Dr. Raphael suddenly recalled his own admonitions about the great white belly. "This time, we don't fool around," he told me.

"Why? Is anything seriously wrong?" I was beginning to get worried.

"We can't tell until she has X-rays. And if there is anything wrong, the less she weighs, the better her chances. And if she needs X-rays, she'll need total anesthesia, and any dog who is under gas is better off without a lot of weight to carry."

"Why will she need total anesthesia? If you X-ray her leg, I can hold her still."

"We'll discuss it if the situation arises. She may be walking good as new in a few days. Meanwhile, put her on a diet immediately. And rub Absorbine Jr. into her leg so the muscle doesn't get atrophied from lack of use."

And so we started the waiting period. Not that time hung heavy on my hands. I was extremely busy with Josephine. First there was her usual supply of vitamins to be given. Then there were the three daily sessions with the Absorbine Jr. And of course there was the necessity of trying to catch little cat naps during my free time. I had our glorious athletic nights to face— alone. Irving had temporarily moved into the den. Josephine and I spent the eventful nights together in the bedroom. And they were eventful, now that I carried out all the action single-handedly. Up and down, up and down. Soon I found myself lying awake, waiting for that gentle tug on my arm. It wasn't that Irving didn't care, but he did have to go to the office, and the way he figured it, *one* of us had to get some sleep.

Meanwhile, due to the frequent applications of Absorbine Jr., Josie was beginning to smell like a gymnasium. But somehow the week passed, and the three of us presented ourselves to Dr. Raphael. He placed Josie on the scale. Twenty-five pounds!

I started to alibi. "What can I do? You have to indulge an invalid. She can't exercise or play ball."

He dismissed my chatter with a worried shake of his head. He was really concerned about her leg. I was to take her home and go through the starvation routine for the rest of the day. No food, not even water after six P.M. Then bring her in at nine in the morning. They would give her total anesthesia and take the X-rays. Irving and I stared at each other.

Irving spoke first. "Doctor, isn't this a little drastic for a sprain?"

"I'd give anything if it was just a sprain," Dr. Raphael answered.

I was alarmed. "What is it?"

"I refuse to say until after the X-rays."

We followed his advice and sat out the waiting period for the X-rays. When we returned, Irving and I were ushered into Dr. Raphael's private office. She had no sprain. She had ruptured the cross ligaments under her kneecap.

He went on to explain that these two ligaments crossed under the knee and gave the knee its flexibility. Once the ligaments ruptured, they popped up and shriveled like broken electric wires. They would never mend or heal. The only course was an operation. They would have to cut down through the entire side of her thigh, find two new ligaments, draw them down, cross them, and connect them under the knee and to the calf. It was a rare operation and had only been in practice the last few years. Only fifty per cent of them were successful—and usually only on young dogs. She had everything against her—age and weight. Irving asked what would happen if we didn't operate.

Well, she would continue to walk on three legs. Soon she might even limp on the bad leg as the torn ligaments had no nerve endings and she would feel no pain. But eventually she'd wear away the cartilage near the kneecap, and then bone deterioration would set in. In extreme cases, the leg had to be amputated.

We were all silent for a moment, then Irving came up with the understatement of all time. "Dr. Raphael, this dog is not just a dog to us."

Dr. Raphael said he had kind of gotten that idea.

"We want to do what's best for her," Irving continued. "We don't want her to suffer through a needless operation if it's going to be unsuccessful. But we can't just sit around and let her lose her leg. If she were your dog, what would you do?"

"I'd operate," Dr. Raphael stated. "Because even if the operation is not successful, she'll limp, but she won't lose the leg. But go home and sleep on it. Go to another doctor if you like, get another opinion."

Irving took command. "We believe in you. If you say operate, okay. Do it tomorrow."

Dr. Raphael shook his head. "It's not that simple. I wouldn't chance operating on her while she is so overweight. Not only is it a hazard to her heart with the anesthesia, but once she tries walking, after the operation, her excess weight would snap the new ligaments before they had a chance to strengthen."

"How much does she have to lose?" This was the first time I had asked the question in all seriousness.

"At least five pounds before I operate. Then I'll chance that she'll drop a few more during recovery."

Five pounds! He saw the look of terror in my eyes. It would take her a year to lose five pounds.

"The time element is very important," he went on. "I'm going to help you. I'll give you a prescription dog food that's very low in calories. She gets half a can a day, and one biscuit in the morning—and that's it! If you stick to it, she should knock off five pounds in one week."

We left with the three-legged Josephine and a crate of prescription dog food.

For the first time there was no fooling around with the diet. To make things easier for Josie, everyone starved. Sarah Lee became a thing of the past. Irving and I had our morning coffee at the drugstore. Every

Yummy and goody was thrown out of the apartment. Signs of warning were posted for chambermaids, valets, and all visitors. We never even ate a cracker around her. Why tantalize the girl?

At first she thought we had all gone crazy. But after a few days she began to look at us with compassion. Being an extremely bright little animal, she figured maybe we were going through a period of terrific financial reverses. After all, it was obvious to her that not only was she starving, but there were no big room service orders coming our way either. In fact she was beginning to wonder if we ever ate. Soon she began to adore the special dog food. After all, it was the only bright spot of her day. She pounced on it like it was caviar. But this one meal a day was only an hors d'oeuvre to her. She was always ravenous. When we went walking, she was constantly on the alert for some stray goody. A piece of chewing gum, half a worm, a lollypop stick—the entire outdoors took on a look of a do-it-yourself smorgasbord to her. Central Park was really the danger spot. Not only did she try to beat those poor pigeons out of their bread crumbs, but she even began to eye the pigeons with a new interest. Like, "underneath those gun-metal feathers they might taste mighty like a chickie."

At the end of the week I put her on the scale. Only two pounds had melted away. I called Dr. Raphael. He was adamant. Not until she got down to twenty pounds.

For two more weeks we continued with the concentration-camp living, punctuated with Josie's beseeching stares. Finally we made the mark. Twenty pounds! I called Dr. Raphael triumphantly. He set the operation for the following Monday.

Sunday night I threw a small party for her. Nothing much, just Josie's most intimate friends—Bea Cole, Anna Sosenko, Joyce, and Last-One. (Because Last-One still professed undying love for the girl.) It was a starving party. Since Josie was facing total anesthesia the following morning, not even water could be served. Everyone brought her a toy and tried to be gay, but it was practically a wake. I almost fainted when I heard Joyce whisper to Irving, "Now Irving, remember, go right out and buy Jackie another dog if Josie doesn't pull through." Irving nodded numbly, I screamed I didn't want another dog, there was no other dog in the world except Josie, everyone said Josie was going to be fine, but no one looked overly confident.

It was a murderous evening. No one had a good time except the guest of honor. She was in excellent spirits. She pranced about on three legs and welcomed each guest. At one point she disappeared. Bea found her in the bathroom devouring the toothpaste. Sure, it was peppermint flavored—in her condition, a real delicacy.

The following morning Irving and I accompanied her to the hospital. Both Dr. Bernard and Dr. Raphael had a final heart-to-heart with us. They were going to keep her under observation for twenty-four hours, then operate. I could call the following day at three in the afternoon. The operation would be over by then. The operation itself would cost two hundred dollars, not counting her ten days of hospitalization.

We barely listened. Money didn't matter at a time like this. The fact that for two hundred dollars we could buy a brand-new poodle with four good legs never entered our minds. Our only concern was for her comfort and health.

I wanted to know about her accommodations after the operation.

"We keep her in a cage," Dr. Raphael explained.

A cage! Irving tried to calm me down. "Jackie would like to see her in a room at Doctor's Hospital with a view that overlooks the river," he explained to the doctors. "Of course I'm more realistic. I know dogs have to be kept in cages. But there are cages and there are cages. We want to spring for the deluxe-type cage." Both doctors stared at him.

"I mean," Irving went on, "if you have a large cage, like maybe one for a boxer, we'll go for that. At least the girl will have nice roomy quarters."

Dr. Raphael explained all the cages were the same size. And Josephine wouldn't feel like doing much exercising during her post-operative period. She would be kept under sedation a great deal of the time.

"Will she have round the clock nurses?" (Naturally this was me.)

Dr. Raphael was probably used to nuts like us. He took this as a normal question. "No. Dr. Bernard and I are here all day. At night there are attendants. And there is one man here who is really too old to do any real work. But he loves dogs. So we keep him just to pet the sick dogs and give them affection. He's been known to sit with a post-operative dog for forty-eight hours."

Then he returned to the operation itself, some little facts we should know. Naturally they had to shave her entire leg. In some cases the hair grew back a different color.

"Like what color?"

"Snow white."

I tried to envision the coal-black Josie with one snow-white leg. Oh well, as long as she walked on it. There was always Clairol. We'd tackle that problem when we came to it.

Dr. Bernard reminded Dr. Raphael to tell us about the playpen. Oh yes, we were to get a playpen. What kind of a playpen? The kind of playpen babies use. When Josie came home, we had to keep her from even attempting to jump off or on any object of furniture for at least six weeks. When we were out, and during the night, the safest way to confine her was in a playpen.

As soon as we left the doctor's office I rushed home and called Sheila Bond who has two small babies. "Do you still have Brad's playpen? I'll need it."

There was a slight silence. Then Sheila said, "Gee, congratulations."

I was too upset to make small talk. "Do you have the pen?" I asked.

"No," Sheila answered. "I gave it away last week. But I'll send over Brad's bottle sterilizer, his carriage, and his scale. I'm so thrilled for you. When is the great event?"

"It's tomorrow, but I won't need the pen for another ten days."

Sheila was silent for a moment. Then she said, "Start from the top. Why do you need a playpen?"

I explained. Naturally she was disappointed, but she said she'd be glad to make inquiries throughout her building. Bea said she'd do the same. But it was Joyce who came through. She had a playpen stored away somewhere that she had gotten when one of her dogs had a bad spine.

Bea Cole was sitting with me when Joyce's chauffeur arrived. He walked in, carrying the biggest playpen I have ever seen and set it up majestically in the middle of the living room.

Bea blanched. "Does this mean that when Josie comes to me for a sleepover, she'll arrive with the vitamins, the tube and the nozzle, and the playpen?" (I could see she was mentally rearranging her living room.)

I explained that the nozzle was a thing of the past, and that Josie would not go on any sleepovers until she was her old healthy self.

Bea sat with me the rest of the day to cheer me up. She came up with little things like, "Now stop worrying. Look how well Peter Stuyvesant did with just one leg." And little things like that. By evening just as she was warming up, launching into famous "double amputees" who had lived useful and happy lives, Irving came home. He took over from there. He took me to three movies. Then we came home and each took two of the red pills. But neither of us slept.

Bea arrived at nine o'clock the following morning. It wasn't that she was worried. She knew Josie had a marvelous constitution and that Dr. Raphael and Dr. Bernard were great surgeons. She had just gotten up early and figured maybe I'd like company.

So we drank coffee and started the vigil. Irving tried to look at the bright side of it. "Just think, we can even have Sara Lee for breakfast this morning without the shiv paw clawing us for it."

We sent out for the Sara Lee. But no one touched it. We just sat and waited until three o'clock, when I could call and learn the results.

30

The Day the Earth
Stood Still

At three o'clock Bea got on the extension phone
and I called Dr. Raphael. She had a pad and was prepared to take down the entire conversation in short-
hand so I could relay it word-for-word to Irving, who
unfortunately had to go to work. Dr. Raphael didn't
sound too cheerful.

"We can't tell whether it's successful or not, Mrs.
Mansfield. But the picture isn't too bright. First of all,
we had a rough time finding any new ligaments. Usually we find them easily and have an abundance left
over. The two we finally managed to get and cross
over, just about made it. Whether it will hold or not,
only time will tell. But there is a great deal of muscle
atrophy since we had to wait so long. And there was
some bone damage. But she came through just fine
and is resting comfortably. You call tomorrow at the
same time and we'll be able to tell you more."

I phoned Irving and read him the entire report taken
down by Bea. There was a moment of silence. Then
Irving said, "I don't understand a goddam word. This
is all double talk. Bea must have goofed somewhere."

I suggested *he* call Dr. Raphael and put on his tape
recorder at the same time for insurance. He said that
was just what he intended to do. Ten minutes later
he called me and played the tape back. Same speech.

"Well, genius, what does it mean?" I demanded.

His voice was small. "I think it means it doesn't look too good for the girl."

The news was pretty much the same the following day. We asked if we could visit her. Dr. Raphael said it would only excite her. It was better to phone each day for a progress report. We phoned five times a day. Bea confined herself to one call a day. Each day the answer was the same. She was in no pain, she was eating a little, they had her on that lovely dietetic dog food.

On the fourth day Dr. Raphael sounded like a new man. "Mrs. Mansfield, you've got quite a dog! Even with a young dog, in a successful operation, the dog will not dare to try to use the foot for weeks. Today we took Josie out of the cage and tried walking her a few steps and she had the guts to try to put that leg down! Of course she couldn't, and probably never will, but what spirit."

I thought of Josie and answered quietly and with complete conviction. "Dr. Raphael, she will get well, and she will walk, because she wants to get well."

He didn't fight me. "I'm a great believer in that too. And this dog obviously loves everything about life. I always say, you get from a dog what you put into them. And it's obvious you and Mr. Mansfield have put eight years of love into this animal. She might make it at that."

And so it went for six more days. Each day Dr. Raphael gave me glowing reports on her character. Not her physical progress. Obviously she had captivated the entire staff with her charm. But it was also clear that in their opinion she'd never be eligible for the Olympics or even be able to chase a senile squirrel.

On the tenth day we arrived to get her. Irving and I felt like new parents about to bring a child home for the first time. (The playpen had been set up in the middle of the living room, and all of her toys were in it. We had even ordered flowers to add a festive note.) Dr. Raphael escorted us into his private office.

"Mr. Mansfield, you've got quite a dog. Quite a dog!" He shook his head in wonderment.

We smiled modestly. Dr. Raphael and Dr. Bernard both beamed as if they shared some exquisite secret.

Dr. Raphael was the first to put it in words. "This morning when we tried to walk her a bit, she put her leg down."

We all stared in wonder.

Dr. Raphael went on. "As I told you, even a younger dog wouldn't chance it, but it's almost as if this dog has figured out that the sooner she walks, the sooner she'll get the hell out of here. It's unbelievable."

Then it was Dr. Bernard's moment of triumph. "And she's lost four more pounds. She's down to sixteen pounds now." Everyone congratulated everyone.

Dr. Bernard continued. "It's the low-calorie dog food that's doing it. I want her to stay on it."

"For how long?" I asked.

"For the rest of her life! I want her down to twelve pounds eventually."

Dr. Raphael agreed. "You have to order it. They don't sell it at stores as it's a prescription diet. We've ordered you a case which you can take home, and whenever you run out, we'll reorder it for you."

I agreed to everything. Irving was eager to write the check. We couldn't wait to see the miracle patient.

"Now I expect that the minute she gets out of here, she'll hold her leg up," Dr. Raphael warned us. "But it's your job to make her walk on it. I don't know how, but you obviously can get through to this dog better than anyone else can. I want you to take her on a short leash and walk her—slowly. On short walks. Be sure to carry her up and down curbs. One slip could tear the whole thing. *Never* let her jump on or off anything for at least three months. But try to make her walk on the leg."

"If you have no success in three weeks," Dr. Bernard added, "bring her in and we'll put weights on it."

"Weights?" Irving and I asked together.

"The muscle is very atrophied. If she doesn't use it, it will get even more so. And the weights will force her to put it down. Because in spite of this dog's age and weight, we can almost swear the operation is completely successful."

Then the attendant brought the patient to us! She let out a squeal when she saw us and covered our faces with kisses. To the average person she looked kind of strange, but to us she was a thing of beauty.

Her right leg and hind quarter had been shaved. A deep, wide, ugly red incision about ten inches long glared through the skin. Without fur, her leg and thigh and right *derrière* was about an inch wide. The other side, fluffed out with her abundant fur, was easily six times the size. But nothing marred the perfection of "That Face." I carried her and Irving toted the crate of dog food.

All the bellboys and personnel at the hotel greeted her with moist affection. I held her in my lap all day and everyone dropped by to greet her. I took her outside for a short walk at least five times and pleaded, "Put the leg down, darling."

To my overwhelming joy, she obliged and actually took two or three steps on it. I knew it was going to be a long pull but that eventually she would get well.

That night I placed her in the playpen on a blanket and explained to her about the leg. She snuggled down comfortably and Irving and I put out the lights and got into bed. Five minutes later I felt a familiar scratch on my hand.

I said in a quiet voice, "Irving, you didn't get out of bed and get on the floor and scratch my hand, did you?"

Irving said he knew I had been through a strain and that I had been just marvelous. I mustn't crack up now.

"Something just scratched my hand again, Irving. And if it hasn't, then I *do* need a straight jacket."

"Like what kind of a scratch?"

"Like Josephine scratches."

He said, "Oh sure, she leaped over the playpen and is at your side."

Nevertheless, he turned on the light. Josephine was hobbling around, wagging her tail in delight. For a moment we all had a staring contest. Then Irving picked up Josephine and replaced her in the playpen. Only this time we sat and watched. We wanted to see her pole-vault over the pen. But Josie did it the easy way. She calmly walked through the bars! The bars were only eight inches apart. We began to inspect Josie. Dr. Bernard and the prescription dog food had done quite a job. Aside from all her fur, there really wasn't much dog underneath. Of course the great white belly would never look good in a bikini, but it had definitely shrunk. Our girl was really rid of her surplus weight. And she was also rid of the playpen.

So Irving returned to the den and I returned to spending my nights as Josephine's personal maid. Not only did I have to lift her up, but she also woke me to inform me when she wanted to be put down.

But I was so thrilled to have her back that I didn't mind losing my sleep, my looks, or my husband to the den. Besides, Irving wrote me notes every morning and called me from the office twice a day—so we didn't ever really lose touch.

31

Stalag 17

ONE DAY, about a week after Josephine's return from the hospital, I came home and found her lying on the couch. She looked so cute and cuddly there that it was a good five minutes before I realized that she had been in the apartment alone, prior to my entrance. *She had sprung to the couch on her own!*

Just as I was digesting this fact, the doorbell rang and Josie leaped off the couch and went dashing down the hall, barking at the top of her lungs. I called Dr. Raphael. He couldn't believe it and said to bring her in immediately.

He shook his head in awe as he examined her. Never had he seen such a rapid recovery. But I must hold her back. She *must* not jump on or off anything for another two months.

Irving moved back into the bedroom, and Josephine and I effected a compromise. Okay, she could leap off the bed by herself because I could see she made a three point landing. But she *must not* jump up. I would lift her. She got the point and during the night she allowed Irving or me to lift her whenever the spirit moved her.

But the tough moments occurred when she brought the ball. She wanted to play. We had to force her to play "roll ball" on the floor. No leaping like Yogi Berra.

A month passed and the hair began to slowly grow

back on her leg. And it was black. The scar disappeared.

In January when she celebrated her eighth birthday the fur on her leg had almost grown in. It was still skimpy looking, but she walked on it almost like old times. And whenever we weren't looking, she'd leap on beds, chairs, anywhere her heart desired.

But Josie realized that her life had changed. No more marshmallow cookies. No doughnuts and bow ties in the morning. No beer at night. But she never complained. Because as I've stated, she's the kind of dog who thinks things out. She decided maybe it was the stock market—she heard talk about the slump. Maybe one of Irving's shows had been canceled. Maybe all of them had been canceled. So she tightened her belt. Because as she saw it, at least she had half a can of prescription slop a night and the one lousy biscuit. But *we* never ate anything. And she was positive of that. Any time we went near the kitchen she dashed after us to make sure we weren't sneaking any hidden Yummies. But she was not the fickle type. She loved us during the rough times with the same devotion that she had shown during the rosy days of chicken livers and hard-boiled eggs.

Of course she figured some day everything would straighten out and she'd go back to the old rich life. Every time she passed the delicatessen she tried to urge Irving inside. She knew liverwurst wasn't too expensive. But when he held out, she swallowed hard, and took it in good grace.

Soon she began to feel it had all been a dream. Those glorious days when she licked the frying pan. She hadn't even seen a frying pan in months. And those wonderful nights when Daddy brought home the roast chicken. Maybe she had just imagined it all. Maybe life had always been low-calorie dog food and one lousy biscuit for breakfast.

But being a philosophical dog she merely shrugged and said, "Well, that's show biz!"

32

How Irving Saved the
Day and Doctor

IN THE SPRING Dr. Raphael and Dr. Bernard gave her the "go" signal. She could play ball, jump on and off furniture—she was completely healed. I nodded and didn't tell them she had been jumping and playing ball for the past five weeks. They were also pleased about her weight. She was down to fifteen pounds. As the attendant took my order for a new case of the prepared dog food, Dr. Bernard handed me a nice shiny bottle.

"Since she is on nothing but this food, I want to find out whether we can safely stick with it, or switch to another preparation. So next week, please bring in an early morning specimen. I want to check her kidneys."

I was pleased with this thoroughness and got into the cab with Josie and the shiny bottle. When Irving came home I told him about the bottle and explained Dr. Bernard's request.

Irving was pleased with his interest but wanted to know just how I proposed to get a specimen from a girl poodle. With a boy poodle you had a sporting chance. You could at least try to tie a bottle to a tree and make a stab at catching a little something. But a girl poodle squats. I called Dr. Bernard and stated my problem.

Dr. Bernard said I had no problem. "When you go to Central Park with Josie, just take along a soup

bowl. When she squats, slide the bowl under her."
(You see everything is simple once you learn the
facts.)

But Irving came up with another poser. Josephine
has her special spot in Central Park. Right on the
grass opposite the benches where fifty or sixty people
sit reading *The New York Times*. Forget the fact
that these people would drop their *Times* and stare as
I stuck a bowl under Josie. Maybe I'd have enough
class to carry off the whole thing and just stare back
at them like: "Some people collect stamps or butterflies. I collect this."

But what would it do to Josephine? She'd think I
was some kind of a nut if I suddenly interfered with
her privacy and slid a cold soup plate under her.

But let's suppose, that being the nice dog she is, she
weathered this intrusion, and after a few false starts,
finally obliged me, figuring maybe I got some special
kind of kick out of this. Then what?

There I am, standing in Central Park, holding her
leash in one hand and the freshly filled steaming soup
plate in the other, being eyed by the fifty or sixty
people who have given up the *Times* to watch my
next move eagerly. What's next on my agenda?

Our hotel is right across the street. It's a very stylish
hotel. They've just put a big new chandelier in the
lobby and raised the rents. Do I sashay into this lobby
carrying the steaming bowl of you-know-what as if
it is a fancy dish from Casserole Kitchen? And suppose
the elevator is crowded?

I called Dr. Bernard again. He said to take a funnel
and the bottle to the park along with Josephine and
the soup plate. After she had obliged me by filling the
plate, then take out the funnel and transfer the con-
tents from the soup bowl through the funnel into the
bottle. (Naturally he can come up with all these answers. He's a college man.)

I explained the simple solution to Irving, but added
that he would have to go along as part of the deal.

This was no longer a one-man operation. He would have to hold the leash as I dived under her with the soup plate.

Irving is also a college man and came up with his set of logistics. He presented his case against Operation Soup Bowl.

1. The fact that some cop might come along and arrest us as a pair of degenerates didn't bother him. He would take any risk for her well-being.

2. He also pointed out that in spite of the weight loss, the great white belly still hung so low that it would be impossible to get a soup bowl under her. Now a flat saucer would be different. But everyone knows you can't collect a really good specimen in a flat saucer.

3. If I did get the bowl under her, then what? Did I squeeze in between two men on the bench, elbow them aside, and set up light housekeeping right there with the bowl of you-know-what, the funnel, and the bottle?

This time Irving called the doctor. He explained that he was sure Josephine had marvelous kidneys and felt that a specimen was not really necessary. Dr. Bernard sounded wounded. They liked to be very thorough with all post-operative cases. But of course if Irving wasn't really interested—

Irving hastily assured him we were very interested. (After all, Dr. Bernard and Dr. Raphael had saved the girl's life. They were the best doctors in town. We couldn't lose them!)

If they wanted a specimen, they'd get it! From here on, he'd take over! And as Irving explained to me, we were really doing this to keep the doctors happy. Not Josephine. So bright and early the next morning, Irving brought them the bottle. And that's how we discovered Irving had a great pair of kidneys!

33

Postscript

IT IS a year and a half since the operation. Josephine is nine and one-half years old, but she leaps, jumps, and acts like a puppy. She is still eating the low-calorie dog food, but like all females, cheats just a little. (Like dinner at Last-One's or a sleepover at Bea Cole's.) Her weight wavers between sixteen and eighteen pounds.

Her friend Moppet is a gentle old lady who rarely comes to the park. She enjoys her twilight years and likes gracious easy living. She has long forgotten her wild weekend with Jackie Gleason and that romantic collie.

Billy and Joyce who adore each other (whether married or divorced) are divorced again. Billy gained custody of the seventh dog, a darling Maltese terrier named Zoey. But he gave Joyce a new gray poodle. She and the gray poodle went to Switzerland. The gray poodle is adorable and very healthy—at the present writing.

Bobo Eichenbaum has moved to New Jersey where he is regarded by the Jersey dogs as an eccentric but likable bachelor, who tells outrageous lies about his fling on television, and his unrequited romance with a glamorous show business girl poodle.

Baby Mayer, the dachshund across the hall, is Josephine's closest buddy-buddy. She adores Josephine and respects her seniority.

But Josie only pulls this seniority rank when she needs it. At heart she is still a girl. She knows she has

a full and active life ahead. And an adventurous one.
Especially now with the wonderful new order of the
day: *Where we go, Josephine goes.*

This innovation took place a few months ago. We
had to go to the Coast for another short trip. Naturally Bea Cole was all puckered up, waiting for her
house guest. It was a lovely day, so Irving and I decided to walk Josie over to Bea's. Josie pranced along
resplendent in a new haircut. Her legs all fluffed out,
ribbons on her ears.

Irving said proudly, "You can't even tell which leg
had the operation."

"Maybe I should tie a ribbon on the bad leg or
something," I suggested.

"What for?"

"So Bea and Karen will remember to take it easy.
After all, that leg still has to be pampered."

"Bea's very good about that," Irving replied after a
long pause.

"Oh, it's not Bea I'm worried about. It's that new
couch she got, and those chairs she had covered."

"What's Bea's furniture got to do with Josie's leg?"
Irving asked.

"Well, the new chairs are covered in satin. Satin is
very slippery. Josie could slip off them. And the new
couch is very high. She might have trouble leaping
on it."

"That's ridiculous," he answered.

We walked a block in silence. Then he said, "How
slippery is satin?"

"I don't know. *I* don't leap on and off it."

Another block of thoughtful silence. Then he said,
"How high is the couch?"

"Pretty high."

He shook his head. "How could Bea do anything
so stupid? She knows satin is slippery."

"It's pretty though," I insisted. "Besides, I'm sure
it will be all right."

He nodded. We walked half a block, then he stopped. "You know damn well I'll worry all the time we're away with that big couch and satin chairs."

I said that unfortunately Bea's decorator hadn't built the place around Josie's leg.

"Well no decorator is going to cripple my dog!" He suddenly hailed a cab and ten minutes later, Josie and I were back in our apartment and Irving was on the phone shouting at all the airlines. "What do you mean she rides in a cage. She sits with us!"

After pleas, threats, and the courtesy of a dog-loving pilot, Josie made it to California. She loved the entire trip. She slept on my lap, with one eye opened, fastened at all times on the hostess. She was determined not to miss one hors d'oeuvre . . . one cookie . . . one meal . . . not even an aspirin. To her the plane was a flying smorgasbord.

In a few months from now, Irving expects to film some television shows in Europe. When he learned that England won't admit dogs and holds them in quarantine for six months, he just shrugged philosophically and said, "Well, that finishes London."

Perhaps you think this is an infantile attitude for a grown man. It might be—for any grown man who has not lived with a poodle. But once you and a poodle have shared the same leash, you're hooked! A certain chemistry seems to flow through that leash uniting both poodle and master. Eventually you aren't even sure whether you are walking the poodle, or the poodle is walking you.

Anyway, that's the way it is with us and Josephine. And once again I am reminded of that sign in a pet shop window. "The Only Love You Can Buy Is The Love Of A Puppy."

It is a tremendous truth. The moment Josephine came to us, she spent every waking moment trying to please us and in loving us.

But there should be an addition to that sign. Because

although you inherit the love of a puppy right from the start, it spends its entire life trying to *earn* your love.

Josephine has more than earned it! They say poodles can do everything but talk. Well, that's fine, because talk is the easiest part of love. The phrase "I love you" is said too easily and too often. Josephine doesn't need to talk. The love that shines from her eyes makes words unnecessary.

You can learn a lot about love from a dog's devotion. At least we have. But unfortunately, we're only human, and no human's love can be as consistent as Josephine's. We can talk, but no language has been invented that can convey to that small bundle of fur the happiness she has added to our lives. Yet we can try, and so we say: "We love you—every morning . . . *every* night, Josephine!"

———

Epilogue

December, 1969

Shortly before he became President of the United States, Richard Nixon looked me in the eye and said, "The difference between a cocker spaniel and a poodle is . . . a cocker is all heart and no brain. A poodle is all brain and no heart. Except Josephine . . . who has both!"

Every *Night, Josephine!* was first published in hardcover on November 14, 1963. And a star was born!

Often when I walked the star in Central Park, someone would come over and say, "Is this *the* Josephine?" I would nod, and the star would wag her tail. (She took her fame beautifully . . . always greeted strange dogs and people with easy charm.) Her fans would stare in mute admiration. But ever so often there was one who would say, "Do you mind if I reach down and touch her?" (We would nod again. To Josephine it was like signing an autograph. Actually she doesn't *like* her head rubbed . . . she prefers it on her belly, but it wouldn't be dignified for a star to lie down and roll over for some belly-rubbing right in Central Park.) Then the fan would rub her head and say, "Oh when I go back and tell my friends that I've met and touched *the* Josephine! Oh Josie, I just loved *your* book." Then they would walk away without even saying goodbye to me.

Josephine took it for granted that every time I sat at the typewriter it concerned her in some way. She felt she had to lie at my feet and 'collaborate.' I didn't dare tell her that *Valley of the Dolls* wasn't a sequel to her book. When she learned the truth, she took it in good grace. But when I sat down to write *The Love Machine*, she was positive that *this* time it *had* to be *her* sequel. Because so much has happened to her since Every *Night, Josephine!* was published. She shared a hair dryer at Poodle Boutique with Victoria Nixon, a small black poodle. (Of course Josephine introduced us to the Nixons. No one just goes around meeting Presidents.) She's been given a cocktail party by the Duke and Duchess of Windsor. (She took Irving and me along.) She was admired and petted by Dame Margot Fonteyn. She was belly-rubbed by one of the Rolling Stones. (She thought he had a marvelous touch.) And as I think about it, I feel she is completely justified. She *should* have a sequel. And I certainly intend to write it one day.

But the entire point of this epilogue is to state that Josephine will be sixteen January 10, 1970, and I am so grateful to be able to say that she is alive and well on Central Park South.

Jacqueline Susann

ABOUT THE AUTHOR

JACQUELINE SUSANN was born in Philadelphia. Her mother was a school teacher and her father was Robert Susann, the famous portrait painter. At the age of sixteen, Miss Susann announced that she wanted to be an actress. Before she had a chance to reconsider, her parents bought her a one-way ticket to New York.

She acted in several Broadway shows, and appeared frequently on television. In 1963, her first book, *EVERY NIGHT, JOSEPHINE!* was published and became an immediate success. It was followed by VALLEY OF THE DOLLS, which rose swiftly to become a worldwide and world-famous bestseller. Her most recent bestselling novel is THE LOVE MACHINE.

Miss Susann is married to television and motion picture producer Irving Mansfield. She divides her time between New York City and California.